Your New Self

How to Use Lies to Manipulate Lies and Create the Life You Desire

Sophie Bui

Copyright © 2025 by Sophie Bui
First Paperback Edition

All rights reserved. No part of this publication may be reproduced, distributed, or transmitted in any form or by any means, including photocopying, recording, or other electronic or mechanical methods, without the prior written permission of the publisher, except in the case of brief quotations embodied in critical reviews and certain other noncommercial uses permitted by copyright law. For permission requests, write to the publisher, addressed "Attention: Permissions Coordinator," at the address below.

Some names, businesses, places, events, locales, incidents, and identifying details inside this book have been changed to protect the privacy of individuals.

Published by Freiling Agency, LLC.

P.O. Box 1264
Warrenton, VA 20188

www.FreilingAgency.com

PB ISBN: 978-1-963701-56-2
E-book ISBN: 978-1-963701-57-9

"I dream of a day when the potential of married couples in this country can be unleashed for the good of humankind, when husbands and wives live life with full emotional love tanks and reach out to accomplish their potential as individuals and as couples. I dream of a day when children can grow up in homes filled with love and security, where children's developing energies can be channeled to learn and serving rather than seeking the love they did not receive at home." —Gary Chapman

Contents

Preface: My Story ix

1 Understand the Inner Lies 1
- Why Do We Have These Inner Lies? 1
- Inner Lies and Emotional Pain 4
- Root Causes of Emotional Pain 4
    - Suppressions: The Hidden Burden 4
    - Assumptions: The Trap of Others' Opinions 7
    - Dishonesty: The Poison 9

2 Unwiring the Pain Circuit 15
- Build Your Fortress 18
    - Seek Mother Nature 21
    - Seek Silence 25
    - Seek Inner Truth 29
    - Seek Reset 32
- Why This Fortress Matters 43

3 How to Use Lies to Manipulate Lies 45
- Define the Act of Manipulation 47
- The Twisted Manipulation 49
- How to Master Self-Manipulation 51
    - Part 1: Weaken the Inner Lies 51
        - Identify the Inner Saboteur 51
        - Get aggressive with the Inner Voice 53

- Repeat the Mantra: Everything Is Just an Illusion 56
    - Part 2: Manipulating Your Own Mind 58
  - Manipulation Strategies 59
    1. When It Tries To Demotivate You 59
    2. When It Tries To Sweet Poison You 60
    3. When It Makes You Feel Unloved or Betrayed 62
    4. When It Makes You Feel Stuck in Regret or Sadness 63
    5. When It Makes You Feel Worried About the Future 64
4 Self: Defining Self-Love, Self-Betrayal, and Selfishness 67
  - Self-Love 69
  - Self-Love vs Self-Betrayal 70
  - Self-Love vs Selfishness 70
  - Practicing Self-Love 74
  - Habits of Self-Love 75
    - No Complaints 76
    - Focusing on Small Wins 76
    - Reflection 76
    - Living Today As Your Last Day 76
    - Committing to Consistent Kindness 76
5 Building An Unbreakable SELF 93
  - Introduction to the Four Dimensions of Life 95
    - **Physical**: "I must treat my body like a temple." 95

- o **Mental**: "No one has the right to define who I am or who I should be." 95
- o **Emotional**: "I am doing my best, and everyone is already trying their best to be happy." 95
- o **Spiritual**: "Everything happens for the best reasons." 95
- Introduction to the Suppleness Power 96
- Establishing an Unbreakable SELF 97

6 Living in the New Me 133
- The True Change of Behavior and Identity 133
  - o Notion of 4 Ms 135
  - o Productivity Quadrant 138
  - o Four Pillars of a Life of Mastery 144
    1. An Organized Mind: The Blueprint for Success 144
    2. Decisiveness: The Power of Taking Action 144
    3. Follow-through: Bridging the Gap Between Dreams and Reality 144
    4. The Mindset of Giving Back: Unlocking Abundance Through Service 145

Final Words 155

Preface

My Story

BEFORE WE DIVE into the ideas, tools, and wake-up calls this book has to offer, I want to start with something more real than any self-help formula: my story. Because if you're anything like me—and I have a feeling you might be—you've been carrying around a mix of ambition and exhaustion, clarity and confusion, power and pain. I didn't wake up one day enlightened. I got here through trial, error, a few faceplants, and a whole lot of reflection.

Like many of you, I was born with dreams, hopes, and some pretty wild delusions about myself. I didn't just think I was special—I *knew* I was special.

My mother was a force of nature—part warrior, part political strategist, part financial wizard, and 100% terrifying when she set her mind to something. At 21, after my grandfather passed, she took command of the family like a general leading an army, securing power, making money, and bulldozing through life with an iron will that didn't tolerate weakness or excuses. She mastered the art of influence, understood that bending the truth was sometimes necessary, and could talk her way into (or out of) anything—all while making sure everyone ate, succeeded, and, of course, knew she was in charge. Then, there was my father—her complete opposite—an intellectual with three degrees and zero interest in power, strategy, or controlling anything beyond his own thoughts. He was an observer of life, a man who believed in flow rather than force, the kind of person who could drop one line of wisdom that would make you rethink your entire existence. And so, I was born into a cosmic tug-of-war—one parent wielding ambition like a sword, the other floating through life like an enlightened monk—and I, somehow, inherited both: my mother's unshakable determination and my father's existential detachment, making me an overachiever who sometimes just wants to sit by a river and question reality.

Growing up in Vietnam, my interactions with my parents were limited due to their demanding government jobs, so my grandmother mostly raised me and my auntie—two women who shaped my world just as much as my parents did. My grandmother, a free-spirited and fiercely independent woman, defied traditions from a young age, once fleeing an arranged marriage on horseback at just 13 years old, and carried that same unyielding nature into old age, ruling our family with a mix of love, stubbornness, and bizarre house rules that made no sense but were always rooted in her deep devotion to family. My auntie, raised by my grandmother, became the silent backbone of our household—never seeking the spotlight, yet holding everything together with unwavering loyalty and care. Then there was my uncle, a rare genius with an extraordinary mind—able to master anything from musical instruments to languages with ease—yet, at just 16, he inexplicably fell into the depths of alcohol addiction, a tragic reminder that brilliance alone is never enough to escape life's darkest turns. Together, they formed the beautiful, chaotic, and deeply imperfect family that shaped me, teaching me that love, no matter how flawed, is always at the core of who we are.

I became a child shaped by fire and air, by logic and chaos. My family didn't just love me; they *bribed* me with affection. And I, being the little mastermind I was, took full advantage.

The result? A tiny dictator with a superiority complex.

I truly believed I ruled the world. Everywhere I went, I left a trail of chaos. I was the family's *official troublemaker*, their daily dose of stress, and the cause of at least

90% of my parents' exhaustion. I had the *hair of a bird's nest*, dressed like a boy, *sweat on my upper lip 24/7*, and always looked like I was ready to pick a fight.

I have a very odd symptom—one that, if I had to guess, most of you probably have too, just not as weirdly extreme as mine. Since I was a kid, I have fiercely believed that I was destined for greatness, a rare gem among mere mortals. But somehow, the dreams were ridiculous, the ones you could imagine. While other kids dreamed of becoming astronauts or billionaires, my first grand ambition in life was to own a street food stall selling beef stew. That was it. That was my legacy. My *beef stew empire*. Hustling. Getting cash into my stomach pouch. Then, somewhere along the way, I upgraded my dream to selling pork at the local market. Yes, you read that right. A power move – becoming a pork queen at the market.

But then… I realized something.

Pork is dead. Fish, on the other hand, is alive. Fish is fun.

So I bought fish and started practicing my dissecting skills at home. I went to fish market to observe my future workplace. And oh dear, those fish sellers were loud and aggressive. They screamed. They cursed. They flung fish across the stalls like weapons. They were so aggressive

My Story

that their insults contained more words than my entire vocabulary. I had one look at that workplace and thought it was time for another career change.

Then I dreamed of becoming the proud owner of a coffee stand—but not just any coffee shop, no, it had to be on the street. Wherever I went, if I saw a cup and something watery, I would mix, pour, stir, and create the most horrifyingly disgusting mixtures ever made. It wasn't coffee. It wasn't even drinkable. It was a scientific experiment gone terribly, terribly wrong. I stirred them dramatically and made a mess. Unfortunately, most of those experiments happened during my father's or mother's important business meetings. So, I got yelled at, and I did not want to be yelled at, so I stopped that career and changed to a more *respectable* one.

A teacher.

I gathered my cousin, aunt, and teddy bears in front of a closet, where I used it as my whiteboard. The teddy bears were the worst students imaginable. They had no participation, engagement, or enthusiasm. I would ask them questions, and they would just sit there, lifeless and disrespectful. So, I whacked them so hard that their plastic eyes popped out. It turned out teaching was expensive. After a few tragic bear casualties, my family asked me to stop.

On to the next dream.

I needed something more… **classy, something more peaceful and elegant.**

Fashion designer.

Yes. That's it. That sounded classy. Sophisticated. Intellectual. A career of prestige. I began drawing my designs, fully convinced I was the next Coco Chanel. The future of haute couture was in my hands. I felt elevated—like I had finally found my calling. But there was just one problem: I had absolutely no talent for it.

My dresses looked weird.

Not just bad—WEIRD.

They had no structure. No logic. They were just too flat. I did not know how to draw the pipe shape for the pants and shirts.

I was mad. Really frustrated.

But for the first time, my parents were so happy. Out of all my scattered, chaotic dreams, this was the one that gave them peace. So, they invested in me. They put me in a drawing class to help me grow my talent.

I was eager. Excited. I prepped my sketchbook, sharpened my pencils, and showed up to my first class fully convinced that in just a few months, I'd be already in a fashion show.

When I went to the first class, the teacher told us to draw a statue. The worst part was that I was asked to draw a proportioned one with a ruler. We had to measure it, use rulers, and make sure everything was balanced. To me, this was unacceptable. My entire life, I had never been able to cut anything straight or evenly. I did not enjoy that cutting activity because it required too much silence and focus, and it dragged my mood down. And now this guy wanted me to use a ruler and draw with precise measurements. This was a nightmare. I struggled, erasing and redrawing, trying to make my statue look proportional instead of lopsided and confused. Then, in the second class, he asked me to draw a tomato. A tomato. Seriously. I looked at my flat, sad pants sketches from before, and now I looked at my disastrous tomato, and I felt rage. That was when I knew. This was not for me. Pure, artistic rage. It killed me. It killed all my enthusiasm, eagerness, dreams, and hopes.

By the third class, I quit.

Fine. If I couldn't draw, then maybe I was born to be a beauty queen. And let me tell you, nobody has ever dreamed of being a beauty queen with more conviction than I did. With my short, bird-nest hair, I faced a serious problem: beauty queens on TV all had long, flowing locks. But I was not one to accept defeat. I grabbed the longest pair of pants I could find and put them on my head. Instant transformation. From an ordinary, short-haired kid to a glamorous pageant queen. To complete the look, I sneaked into my aunt's room, rummaged through her makeup, and painted my face like I was ready to hit the Miss Universe stage. My aunt's makeup was destroyed, and my parents looked at me speechless.

I didn't stop there.

I decided that being a queen was not a solo journey. So, I recruited my other aunt into my beauty empire. I grabbed her, forced her into my world, and gave her a full makeover . And when we were finally glammed up, we didn't just sit there admiring our beauty. No. We performed. I set up a fake interview, channeling my best TV host energy.

"Miss Universe, please tell us—what is your secret to beauty?"

"Miss Universe, how do you feel winning the crown?"

We spoke with elegance, we waved like royalty, we answered in our most serious beauty queen voices.

My Story

And when I got bored with that, I moved to another game.

Mafia Boss.

I turned to my cousin, my most loyal recruit, and told her: *"We need to start a business. A serious one."* And where did all the best criminal masterminds strategize their empire?

In the bathtub, obviously. We climbed into the tub and initiated high-level discussions about our underground empire. "The deals. The secrets. The strategies. The expansion plans." We whispered in hushed voices, making sure no one overheard our confidential operations. We had a vision. A dream.

My entire childhood, if I wasn't bossing my aunt and cousin around, I was terrorizing my dad, my mom, and the *entire* neighborhood. Every day was an opportunity to *cause problems on purpose.*

I once *rang all the neighbors' doorbells* and ran away, convinced I had just pulled off the greatest heist in history.

I *convinced my cousin to steal fish from the neighbor's pond* so we could raise them ourselves then returned them after when they became grownups.

And my proudest moment? Designing a *mouse parachute*. My cousin and I thought we were *geniuses*. We put a mouse in a bag, attached our "parachute," and launched it off a *four-story building* to "save its life."

In short, I was a walking contradiction. A hyperactive, delusional, chaos-loving kid with a mind so scattered it could never settle on one thing. I just needed to do things—whatever things I could think of, with whoever was crazy enough to hang out with me.

And when I say crazy, I mean it. I was a menace.

I didn't just play games—I created them. One time, I came up with a game with the kids in my mom's company: Building a fancy graveyard for a dead bee. We handpicked all the beautiful flowers and plants from my mom's company for this graveyard (which was, obviously, off-limits) and arranged them in an elaborate cemetery. We prayed. Seriously prayed. After that, I got caught and faced the wrath of adults. I tried to negotiate my way out of trouble by attempting to sell my father to the director's wife.

Then, I rallied a group of kids to climb onto my neighbor's rooftop and open an illegal hair salon. Armed with a pair of kitchen scissors and zero experience, I convinced my friends that I was an expert stylist and proceeded to butcher everyone's hair. After that haircut session, they all looked like they had electric shocks.

My Story

Looking back, I have never had a single normal day in my life. I thrived on annoying people, disrupting peace, and creating absolute chaos. If there was calm, I disrupted it. If there was silence, I filled it. I remember being so hyperactive and naughty that every single adult in my life had a personal vendetta against me. I was the kid that, no matter where I went, grown-ups would gather just to tease me, to provoke me, to watch me explode into a fiery, dramatic rage. And I never disappointed. I had zero tolerance for mediocrity, injustice, or being messed with—a personality trait that, to this day, remains deeply embedded in my character.

A Life of Beautiful Delusions

So yes, my childhood was a *mix of questionable decisions, misplaced confidence, and straight-up delusion.*

But let's be honest—we *all* had our *delusional* moments growing up, right? Maybe you thought your crush was in love with you because they borrowed your pen. Maybe you believed you were *meant* to be famous. Maybe you planned an entire *wedding* in your head with someone who didn't even know your name.

My childhood was chaotic, but if you asked me, I'd tell you I was one of the luckiest kids on earth. Most kids only dream of the kind of freedom—the freedom to wander, ask questions, and challenge anything and anyone I wanted. I wasn't afraid of my voice. I was raised in a family where everyone was civilized, where I was allowed to be fully myself. I was rebellious, curious, a little too wild, but no one tried to tame me. That was the greatest gift my family ever gave me.

In the middle of that freedom, there was something else. A shadow that lurked in the background. A force that I didn't understand but that ruled our household in a way no one could control. My uncle's alcoholic addiction. I didn't have the words for what it meant back then. I just knew that days he was himself—talking, laughing, full of life—and days he became someone else entirely. Eyes half-open, lost in a haze. Drifting through the house like he didn't belong in this world. When he was sober, my family breathed again. The house was alive, filled with warmth and hope. But when he was drinking, the atmosphere turned cold. Heavy. Unbearable. I used to watch him stumble up and down the stairs, his body swaying, his face blank, and something inside me ached.

I didn't know what it was. I just knew I wished he were different.

My Story

The cycle never ended. He would be sober for a while, and then, just like that, he'd disappear again. Some nights, my parents had to hunt him down, searching the city like he was a missing person. Other nights, strangers knocked on our door, demanding money because he had borrowed and vanished. The worries felt endless. The anxious knots in our stomachs tightened every time my uncle left home to drink. We all feared the sound of the door shut, and an invisible clock started ticking in my head. *How long would he be gone this time? Will he come back tonight? Tomorrow? Next week?* And then, there were the women. The ones he would bring home out of nowhere, drunkenly introducing them to the family as if he were living a different life. The house was never quiet during those times. The air felt *heavy*, like it carried the weight of all the unspoken fears, the what-ifs, the worst-case scenarios we played over and over in our minds. The yelling, the blaming, the desperate attempts to make sense of it all—*Why is he like this? Why can't he just stop? What's wrong with him?* The words shot like arrows between family members, but they never landed anywhere useful. Nothing ever changed. My uncle left, my family fought, and the cycle repeated.

And then, there was my mother. The unshakable pillar of our family, the one who carried the weight of it all. She worked endlessly, stretching herself thin to hold our home together, but there were cracks—cracks I noticed even as a child but didn't fully understand until much later. There were nights when I woke up to find her staring at the ceiling, eyes wide open, lost in thoughts she never spoke aloud. I still remember those moments vividly—the room felt cold, I was terrified, but I didn't ask. I didn't dare. I simply watched, frozen in my own helplessness, wondering what kind of thoughts could keep her awake like that. In those days, I saw her hands tremble, restless and anxious as she searched for the house keys, moving in frantic motions. My uncle had a habit of sneaking out, disappearing into the night to drown himself in alcohol, and she was desperate to stop him. So, we hid the keys, locked every door, and lived in a state of constant vigilance. It was like living in a war zone where the enemy was someone we loved. And then there were the times we locked him up. Six months. Six months of keeping him confined to his room, delivering food to him like he was a prisoner in his own home, because what else could we do? What do you do when love isn't enough to stop someone from destroying themselves? What do you do

My Story

when every method—pleading, reasoning, threatening, praying—fails? You do what you think is the last option. But addiction doesn't work that way. It waits. It lurks. It builds up like a pressure cooker, and when the door finally opens—when the leash finally snaps—it comes back worse than before. And my mother—my mother—her patience had an expiration date. When it came, it exploded. The yelling, the screaming, the breaking of things—her rage was a force of nature, a wildfire that no one could stop once it started. The woman who carried so much pain inside of her, who bottled it up in the name of survival, would let it out in terrifying, uncontrollable waves. And I, a child watching it all, had no choice but to sit in the middle of the storm, hoping it would pass. The worst part? It always passed. And then, it would begin again. A cycle. A never-ending loop of suffering, screaming, silence, and waiting. I grew up knowing that pain and betrayal had a rhythm. They are always there. That chaos had a pattern. And no matter how much I wished for peace, it slipped through our fingers the moment we thought we had it. There were nights I sat in my room, numb, listening to the sound of my mother breaking. It was sudden and disastrous. The ugliest of this kind of experience is that it's from the people you love; it's the mix of feelings of disappointment and distrust, and I felt like I was a useless person. And then it would begin. The clash of glass shattering against the floor. The sharp, unrestrained cracks in her voice as she screamed—words that didn't even sound like words anymore, just raw emotion, spilling out after being held in for too long.

And then, the moment that terrified me the most—her body giving up.

I didn't understand seizures. I didn't know what was happening medically, but I knew what I was witnessing. It wasn't just stress. It wasn't just anger. It was something deeper, something that went beyond words, beyond arguments, beyond whatever she was yelling about. This was what happened when pain had nowhere else to go. It was as if all the suffering she had endured, all the years of toxicity, betrayal of trust had forced its way out in the only way it knew how. And the body gave up.

I went to the temple and prayed. I prayed for my uncle to change, for my family to stop suffering, and for the pain to go away. But my prayers were met with nothing. After a while, I stopped believing in them and learned to distrust my own family members.

Throughout my childhood, I studied my uncle's face and learned to detect the shift. When his eyes looked too tired, his voice sounded too slow, and the air in the house became too quiet, that was when I knew we were heading into winter.

Many times, I asked him, "*Uncle, are you addicted to alcohol?*". He said: "*No, I am not addicted; I am just drinking for fun*". But nothing about this looked like fun to me; I knew he was sad—I could see it in the way he moved, the way his eyes never truly looked at us, even when he was standing right in front of us. No one *wants* to be sad. No one *chooses* to wake up every day and destroy themselves piece by piece. I knew that. But then *why* did he keep doing it? Why did he keep falling back into the same cycle, over and over again, knowing it would only lead to pain?

And I know I'm not the only one.

You've felt it too, haven't you? Maybe in your family, in a friendship that turned cold, in a love that shattered when you thought it never could. Maybe in a moment of betrayal so sharp it stole the breath from your lungs. Or in a quiet disappointment that slowly, over time, turned into something heavier than you ever imagined carrying.

Life has a way of showing us its cruelest corners when we least expect it. Of reminding us that nothing is promised, that people change, that love can break, that trust is not always returned in the way it is given. We all walk through life carrying wounds—some fresh, some decades old, but all etched into who we are. And no matter how different our stories may seem; pain speaks the same language.

Betrayal doesn't just hurt—it hardens us, teaching us to guard ourselves so fiercely that even love struggles to get in. Disappointment breeds resentment, making us question everything we once believed in. Failure whispers shame, convincing us we are not enough, that we never will be. Regret traps us in the past, keeping us frozen in a story we can't rewrite. Loss strips us of faith, making the world feel empty and unfair. And then there's the silence. The endless mental loops—what if, why, how did it end up like this? Some of us try to untangle the knots, dissecting every moment, searching for answers that may never come. Others try to outrun the pain, drowning it in work, in distractions, in anything that will keep it at bay for just a little longer.

For me, the events that happened to me were beyond my control, towering over me like waves too high to escape. I couldn't change them. I couldn't fix them. I could only *wait*. Wait in silence, wait for the storms to pass, wait for the shouting to stop, for the crying to fade, for things to go back to *normal*—whatever that meant. And I craved, craved for power, so I would never be powerless again. I would never let anything control me and my family again. I would never let us be at the mercy of something we couldn't stop. One day, I will be so powerful that I will pull my family out of this hell.

The Goodbye That Changed Everything

Life has a funny way of flipping everything upside down just when you think you've figured it all out. One moment, I was ruling my little kingdom in Vietnam. Then suddenly, one day I was told: *You're leaving. You're going to Canada to study.* At first, I was excited. Canada! A whole new world, new opportunities, new adventures! But deep inside me, an unfamiliar sadness started creeping in, like a quiet whisper that got louder as the days counted down. I didn't understand it then, but my soul *knew*—this wasn't just a trip. This was *goodbye* to the world I had always known.

The day I left home, my cousin—my uncle's daughter—hid under the stairs and cried. She had always been there, woven into my life like an unspoken presence, but I had never truly *seen* her. She was my sister in every way that mattered, yet I had spent most of our time together resenting her without fully understanding why. Maybe because I had always received more of it in a home where love often felt scarce. Maybe because, despite the chaos that ran through our family, I had a sense of security she never had. Her childhood was not just unstable—it was a battlefield. Her father was an alcoholic, slipping in and out of consciousness, never fully present, never truly *there*. Her mother, though strong and dedicated, was emotionally hardened, incapable of offering warmth. And between them was my cousin, navigating a world that gave her no space to be a child. She had already learned not to expect tenderness, not to rely on anyone, not to ask for things that were never freely given to her. She was quiet and withdrawn but had a quiet rebellion simmering beneath the surface.

I never truly understood her.

She didn't share much. She didn't cry in front of me. She didn't explain her pain, and I didn't ask. And then, on the day I left, she broke. Tucked beneath the stairs, her body shook with silent sobs. It was the first time I had ever seen her so vulnerable, so open, so… *small*. For the first time, I realized just how much I had taken her for granted. For years, I had been so consumed with myself, with my own desires, my own insecurities, my own struggles, that I never stopped to wonder what it was like to be *her*. And now, I was leaving. Leaving her behind in the very place I had always longed to escape. I stood there, gripping my suitcase, and felt something inside me ache in a way I had never felt before. The guilt, the regret, the unspoken *I wish I could go back to the times we were together*…that I couldn't say.

Upstairs, my grandmother was breaking, too. Her frail hands clutched the railing as if it were the only thing keeping her upright. She wept so hard she could barely stand, and in the midst of her sobs, she reached for me, slipping something into my hand.

It was $2,000—her life savings.

She pressed it into my palm like it was a final act of love, a silent plea to take care of myself in a world she couldn't follow me into.

I stepped onto that plane carrying *all* of it with me.

At 14 years old, my world flipped. One moment, I was somebody—the leader, the center of attention, the girl who walked into a room and owned it. The one who had never been afraid to make the rules, create the games, chase after whatever she wanted, and express whatever she loved. The firecracker. The storm. The girl who knew she was meant for something big.

And then, overnight, I became nobody.

My parents sent me to Canada for a better future, but they never warned me about the emotional free fall that came with it. No one told me how it felt to lose yourself completely. No one told me that "a better future" meant walking into a new world where I had no voice. In Vietnam, I had confidence. In Canada, I had silence. In Vietnam, I was the leader. In Canada, I was invisible. I went from being seen to being overlooked. From being known to being unknown. From walking into a room like I belonged there to stepping into class every morning with a weight in my chest, hoping no one noticed me struggling to understand what the teacher was saying. The girl who used to command attention now avoided eye contact. The girl who used to speak her mind now measured every word, terrified of mispronouncing something and looking stupid. The girl who used to create the rules now sat at lunch with no one to sit with, no one to talk to, pretending she was busy just so people wouldn't see how alone she was. I had been somebody. Now, I was no one.

In Canada, I moved in to live with my other aunt and her family. There are five of us in our family, crammed into an old three-bedroom condo, rationing food, trying

My Story

to keep up with bills. My aunt worked endlessly, yet we barely scraped by, trying to make ends meet. I watched my aunt come home from work exhausted, drowning in responsibilities, and I learned to gauge her mood before speaking. If she were happy, I could breathe. If she were stressed, I stayed out of sight. And I didn't realize it at the time, but I was being trained—I was learning that my worth, my comfort, my safety depended on someone else's emotional state. I became very careful. Careful not to take up too much space. Careful not to say the wrong thing. Careful to be exactly what was expected of me. I adapted. I made myself smaller, quieter. At school, I wasn't the leader anymore—I was the girl in the background. At home, I didn't speak up; I just observed, constantly lied, and became extremely cautious with everything. I learned how to please, how to accommodate, how to survive under someone else's roof. And I didn't realize it at the time, but I was being very skillful at faking.

Like each and every one of us, as we grow up, we begin to shed parts of ourselves. We strip away our wildness, our laughter, our loudness. We learn to adapt. We learn to lie, to stay silent. And I was no different. I lost myself when I didn't even know I was losing…It happens so slowly and naturally…

Coming to Canada was the first time I stepped outside the safety net of my family, the first time I was truly alone in a world that didn't recognize me, and the first time I understood just how much of life was built on suppressions—hiding, lying, assuming, not only those that people tell outright, but the ones whispered in between words, the ones that exist in silence, the ones we craft with our actions, the ones we tell ourselves because facing the truth is just too painful.

Coming to Canada didn't just force me to adapt—it pushed me into the deepest layers of human psychology. It made me hyperaware of how people interacted and how they responded, what made them like someone, and what made them drawn to one person over another. I wasn't just surviving anymore; I was studying, refining, and perfecting the art of influence. I learned quickly that lying wasn't always malicious; sometimes, it was a necessity. I told lies not because I wanted to deceive, but because it made life easier, because it kept the peace, because it was a way to control how others perceived me. I learn to read people effortlessly, to pick up on their emotions, to track their behaviors, to understand what made them tick before they even realized it themselves. I knew exactly what to say to make people like me, to

My Story

make them trust me, to make them feel seen and heard, to make them choose me over someone else. I understood when to speak and when to stay silent, when to play along and when to push back, when to be agreeable and when to be firm—and because of that, I became exceptional at influencing outcomes, at shaping my environment and getting what I want. And I told lies to my parents back home, to my aunt in Canada, to soothe her mood, to avoid her anger, to make sure I didn't add to her stress, because I knew how hard she worked to provide for me. I carefully filtered what I shared with them so they wouldn't worry, because I didn't want them to know how hard it was for me to fit in, how lonely I felt, how much I struggled in silence. I told lies to my teachers, to my classmates, to myself—because pretending was easier than admitting I didn't always have it together. And the thing is—I was good at it.

These tactics became weapons in my arsenal. I knew when to withhold emotion to make someone chase me. I knew when to soften my tone to make someone trust me. I knew when to hold eye contact just a little longer to create intrigue. I knew when to laugh at someone's joke—not because it was funny, but because it made them feel good about themselves. I knew when to say something vulnerable, not because I wanted to, but because it would make the other person feel closer to me. I was pulling strings without anyone seeing them. The truth is, we all do this to some extent—we all adjust ourselves in different settings, we all shape our interactions to get what we want, we all adapt. But I wasn't just adapting anymore. I was controlling. I had turned my emotions into tools, into levers I could pull at will. If I wanted someone to feel something, I knew exactly what to do. If I wanted someone to act a certain way, I could influence that, too.

My best friends would jokingly call me fake, and I laughed it off. After all, wasn't this a strength? Wasn't this an asset? It's called soft skills, wasn't it? Being able to say the right thing, at the right time, to the right person—it got me ahead, didn't it? I thought of it as a gift—an asset, a skill that allowed me to move through life with ease. It took me years to realize that every perfectly crafted sentence, every polite smile, every time I shaped myself to fit what others wanted—was quietly stripping me of something sacred: my true self. The purest soul that God placed in me to shine in this world was dimming. What I once believed was my greatest strength—my ability to adapt, to please, to perform—had become a mask I couldn't take off. Then it became my second nature. I wasn't just telling lies—I was living them. I had lost track of authenticity and genuine intentions without even knowing it.

I studied *coolness* like it was a survival skill. If I could make the popular kids at school laugh *just once* that day, then it would be a *good day*. Those moments—those fleeting, insignificant reactions—became my lifeline. I felt *disconnected* in a way that I could no longer explain. A kind of loneliness that didn't just sit in the background but lived in me, stitched into my every thought, my every movement.

But I had a mission: *Do not fail.*

Eventually, I became the girl who could do it all, who didn't need help, who thought she had everything figured out. I became so stubbornly firm on this belief.

The only thing that made sense to me was power. Power over everything.

I believed that if I could accumulate enough wealth, enough influence, enough control, I could change everything that had ever broken me and my family. I could turn impossible into possible. I could make things right. I imagined we could live happily together in a peaceful life, with no more goodbyes, no more fears, no more tears, no pains, no worries, and no more insecurities. I imagined a life where my mother never had to collapse from exhaustion or grief, where she never had seizures from stress that had nowhere else to go. I imagined a life where I had a say, where I wasn't just the powerless observer in my own life.

I believed—if I just worked hard enough, if I just became enough, I could fix it all. Because if power meant never having to feel helpless again, then I wanted all of it.

That's why I became *obsessed*.

I buried everything behind me. My fears, my loneliness, my exhaustion—I stuffed them down, locked them away. I had no backup plan. No room for failure. I convinced myself that *success* was the only way to erase the shame of struggling. If I worked *hard enough*, if I grinded *relentlessly*, and if I became *somebody* again, I would finally be safe. Safe from failure. Safe from judgment. Safe from the fear that had followed me my entire life—the fear of *not being enough*.

So, I did what I always did.

I outworked everyone. I pushed harder. I manipulated more.

I worked 12 to 16 hours straight—no breaks, no complaints. During university, I juggled full-time classes with four to five shifts a week at work. I barely slept. I barely had time to think.

My Story

I was starving for success. For belonging. For recognition. For approval. For admiration.

Then one day, my aunt's marriage collapsed under the weight of something that had been building for years. It didn't happen overnight—it unraveled in slow motion, one exhausting day at a time, until there was nothing left to hold it together. The reason? She was tired. Tired of carrying the weight of a life that felt like an uphill battle, tired of shouldering responsibilities that never seemed to ease, tired of working herself to the bone while my uncle remained… comfortable. I was too young to fully understand the complexities of marriage, but I knew this: the distance between them wasn't caused by a single event—it was caused by life itself. My aunt had been climbing for so long, and my uncle had stayed behind. She had fought, hustled, pushed forward relentlessly, and she couldn't understand why he didn't have the same fire inside him. The break wasn't about love—it was about survival and growth. Being an immigrant in Canada is not a story of fresh starts and endless opportunities like people back home imagined—it's a battle. A daily, grinding, unrelenting battle to make it, to secure even the most basic stability, to keep up with a system that was never designed for you to succeed. My aunt knew that better than anyone. She arrived with nothing—not the language, not the connections, not the safety net. But she worked. God, she worked. She poured everything into survival, into building a life that was solid enough to stand on its own. She made good money. She bought a house. She achieved the kind of financial security that many immigrants do not reach.

But it came at a cost.

Because for my aunt, life had *only* been about climbing. About pushing forward with no room for rest, no space to slow down, no time to look back. It was about the exhaustion of trying to pull someone up a mountain they don't even want to climb. It was about sacrifice, and the realization that maybe not everyone wants the same things. Her divorce shattered the fragile stability we had. We had to move out to another place. I remember my 10-year-old cousin sitting on the couch in that new place, instead of jumping and exploring the new house, his small frame sinking deeper into the cushions as if he was trying to disappear. He didn't cry out loud—he just sat there, staring blankly ahead, his body tilting slightly to the side, as if the weight of his pain was too much for him to hold up. His eyes were swollen—not in the way a child's eyes should be after crying, but in the way adults

My Story

are when life has crushed them under its weight. There was something haunting in his gaze, something too heavy for a ten-year-old to carry. It wasn't just sadness; it was exhaustion, the kind that comes from overthinking, from replaying moments, from trying to make sense of something that would never make sense. His face had lost the softness of childhood. The brightness, the playfulness—gone. Instead, his expression carried the dull, distant look of someone who had already learned that life could be unfair. That people leave. That nothing is promised. He sat there, his small body sinking into itself, as if trying to disappear into the silence. And now I watched my cousin sobbing, raw, shaking, as if he was begging the universe to undo it. It was as if, in between gasps, he was trying to hold onto every memory of his parents together, rewind time, and force himself back into those happy moments. His sobs sounded like regret. Like somehow, in his tiny, innocent mind, he thought it was his fault. I felt so powerless. I watched him, feeling something inside me twist, tighten. He was just a boy, but at that moment, he looked like someone far older, someone who had seen too much and felt too much. It was as if, overnight, he had stepped into a different world—one where innocence had no place, where love could be taken away without warning, where home could shatter in an instant. And that look—God, that look—it was the look of someone trying to hold themselves together when everything inside them was falling apart. I watched him, knowing he was in unbearable pain but unable to fully understand it myself. My parents were happy together—I had never known this kind of loss. I could feel the way his tiny shoulders trembled, the way his breath hitched every few moments as if his body was trying to hold itself together. And I could feel, most of all, the terrifying stillness—the way he just sat there, barely moving, as if shifting even an inch would break him completely. I didn't know what to say. I didn't know how to comfort him.

That was the part that killed me. That silent, invisible guilt that no child should ever carry.

I started to wonder about the trade-offs in life, about the weight of sacrifices, the depth of pain, the inevitable suffering, and the impossible choices we must make. Where is the right answer? Is there even a right answer?

My Love Life

And in my mid-twenties, I fell in love. Not just any kind of love—the kind that shakes you, strips you, forces you to see the parts of yourself that you've been avoiding your whole life. The kind that makes you question everything you thought you knew about relationships, about yourself, about what it means to truly love and be loved. He was four years younger than me, free-spirited, untamed, carrying an effortless coolness that made people turn their heads. His long hair was always tied up, and his fashion sense was impeccable—he was the kind of guy who didn't follow the world's rules; he created his own. A genius in the coding world, an entrepreneur who had already built success for himself, earning both his bachelor's and master's degrees in software engineering in just four years. Out of all the people I talked to, he was different. There was something about him—his energy, the way he moved through the world, the way he made me feel at home the second I met him. And just like that, Vancouver became a love story, filled with the kind of moments you don't just live—you feel. But love, no matter how beautiful, will always test you. It will reveal the gaps between who you are and who you pretend to be. I had never truly committed to a relationship before. I had an avoidant attachment style, the kind that kept me one foot in, one foot out. I loved unpredictably, with a recklessness that was exciting but unstable. I was the wind—wild, ever-changing, uncatchable. And he? He was the earth—steady, grounded, reliable. His love was consistent, patient, and unwavering. Mine was passionate, chaotic, and consuming. And together, we clashed in a way that neither of us could walk away from.

He was my mirror. Where I was restless, he was calm. Where I avoided, he leaned in. Where I fluctuated, he remained. But beneath that surface of connection, there was an undercurrent of tension, of misalignment, of something neither of us could name but both of us could feel. But my mother kept pressing me to return to Vietnam, calling me every day, her voice layered with urgency and worry, telling me that my grandmother was sick and that the family needed me. But I knew the truth—this wasn't just about my grandmother's health. My mother never liked the life I had built in Canada. She didn't like my job because it did not have a high status, and she didn't see any long-term growth in the way I was living. Though that time was the happiest time of my life, I didn't stop to process my emotions, didn't pause to ask myself what I truly wanted. I was anxious, restless, caught in the inescapable pull of my mother's expectations. So, I made the decision the way I had learned to make all my biggest decisions—fast, detached, efficient. Not slowly. Not thoughtfully. Not emotionally. I executed it like a business deal. I decided to return the keys to my apartment a few weeks later. I didn't consider what I was leaving behind, didn't allow myself to feel the weight of the change. I was always good at pushing forward, ignoring discomfort, and making choices that looked right on the surface without questioning if they were truly right for me. At that moment, it felt like the logical thing to do. But logic has a way of betraying the heart. And I didn't realize it yet, but this decision—the way I left, the way I detached, the way I executed my own departure as if it were nothing more than a task to be completed—was about to teach me one of the most painful lessons of my life.

I told him I was moving back to Vietnam. There was no discussion. I simply returned the house key, declared my departure, and, in my mind, it was done. Because I had already planned this. If he loved me, he would follow me. That's what I told myself. But when I told him, his reaction unraveled me. He was hurt, confused, and betrayed. And then he said the words that would haunt me for months: "If you knew you were leaving, why did you even date me?"

That question made me silent. It pierced straight through me. It shattered every justification I had built up in my mind, every lie I had told myself to make my actions seem reasonable. And for the first time, I saw my own manipulation staring right back at me. I was just like my mother. The way she had convinced me to leave Canada by telling me my grandmother was sick—the way she had carefully woven words together, not to tell the truth, but to create a path toward what she wanted. That's exactly what I had done to him. I had orchestrated the outcome I wanted, not out of love, but out of control of outcomes. After days of silence between us, I decided to end things permanently in the cruelest way possible—I asked him if he was planning to marry me. It wasn't a genuine question. It was a trap. I knew he would say no. He was young, still exploring, still figuring out his future. But I wanted to hear him say it. Because then, I could walk away with the illusion of being the one who was rejected, rather than the one who had destroyed something real. And he only kept silence.

A few days later, I saw him with another girl. I knew before I even saw them. It was a feeling, a gut instinct, the kind that women always have but sometimes choose to ignore. I was walking down the street near my house, and as I approached our ramen place—the one I had

My Story

introduced him to—I saw him standing outside, waiting for a table, with her.

She was into him. I could see it in her body language, in the way she looked at him with admiration, with curiosity, with the kind of hopefulness that I had once carried. But he wasn't looking at her the same way. I stopped. And then I did something I never thought I would do. I walked straight up to them. Smiling. The brightest, most effortless smile I could conjure. I looked at her first. "Are you his girlfriend?" She blushed. She was happy. She liked him. He looked at me, perplexed, caught off guard, scrambling for words. He started introducing her, fumbling over his words—but before he could even finish, I smiled again and looked her dead in the eyes. "Nice to meet you. I'm his ex. This was our spot."

And then, I walked away. I didn't cry. I didn't collapse. I went straight to a bookstore, sat down, and felt nothing. Until the numbness started to fade. Then came the extreme shame. The regret. The betrayal. Then came the nights of hoping he would come back. Then came the days I woke up wishing it was all just a bad dream.

The Great Unraveling

For months. I couldn't eat. I couldn't think. I was grieving—not just him, but the realization of who I had been in that relationship. I had played a game, and I had ost. It wasn't love. It was control. It was manipulation. It was a transaction disguised as a connection. That breakup didn't just break me. It exposed me. It made me see the masks I wear, the small lies that build into bigger lies, the way I manipulate without even realizing it—until the moment it all crumbles. That's why I'm writing this book; I'm not the only one who has done this because we live in a world that teaches us how to win, not how to love. Because if we don't wake up, we will keep hurting the very people we want to hold close. I was blessed to learn this truth. I have learned through this rock-bottom experience—the kind of lessons that don't come from easy days or comfortable choices, but from being stripped bare, from losing everything I thought I knew, and from standing at the edge of myself with nowhere left to run. I will show you how to effectively strip away the lies we tell ourselves—the quiet, insidious ones that shape our decisions, our fears, our relationships, and our sense of self. Because here's the truth: We have been absorbed by lies (the should and should not) about ourselves and

My Story

everything else in life, which makes us fear, and then we start to tell lies to ourselves, that's where the birth of mental prison and conformity. I will take you through that process—the unlearning, the peeling away, the detox of the old identity that no longer serves us. Because if we do not clear out the old, there is no room for the new to enter.

The day I walked away from that ramen shop, smiling on the outside while something inside me collapsed beyond repair, I didn't know that I was about to enter the darkest, most revealing chapter of my life, the kind of chapter that strips you down so completely that you no longer recognize yourself, the kind that forces you to confront every falsehood you've ever told, not just to others, but to yourself, the kind that makes you question whether you have ever truly loved, to the comfort of manipulation, to the false security of knowing exactly how things will unfold because you have orchestrated them to go exactly the way you wanted. For weeks, I was stuck in a haze, floating somewhere between denial and despair, waking up every morning with the same desperate, sinking feeling, that irrational hope that maybe—just maybe—the past few weeks had been nothing more than a bad dream, that if I opened my phone, I would see a message from him, that if I stepped outside my apartment, he would be waiting at my door, looking at me the way he always did, telling me that none of this had to be real, that we could just go back to before, to the warmth, to the safety, to the bubble I had built around us where nothing had to change unless I wanted it to.

But he wasn't there, and there was no message. Slowly, reality began to set in—the sharp, inescapable truth that I had not just lost him, but I had lost something far deeper, something I couldn't yet put into words, something that had been unraveling for years but had only just now revealed itself completely: the truth of who I really was, the truth of how I had moved through life, the truth of how I had always managed to get what I wanted, not through honesty, not through raw vulnerability, but through carefully calculated words and actions, through unspoken power plays, through the delicate but ruthless art of ensuring that every situation, every relationship, every moment bent itself to my will. The most terrifying realization of all was that I had not done this out of malice; I had not done it because I wanted to achieve my goals, not our goals. For the first time in my life, I had to sit with myself, stripped of every mask, every strategy, every carefully curated version of who I thought I needed

My Story

to be, and ask myself the hardest questions about my true self. And I didn't have an answer for the first time in my life. No plan, no backup strategy, no way to outthink or outmaneuver the mess I had created.

So, I did what any person drowning in heartbreak and existential crisis does—I searched for one. I threw myself into books, devouring them like they were the last lifeline left in the world. When you're drowning, you don't think. You don't plan. You just search for something—anything—to grab onto. It doesn't matter if it's sturdy, if it will hold you up for long, if it will truly save you. You just need something to keep you afloat, even temporarily, to stop yourself from slipping under completely. And as I read, as I reflected, as I sat in the uncomfortable stillness of being alone with myself, a realization began to form, not suddenly, but slowly, like a fog lifting just enough to see the outlines of something I had never noticed before: I needed get my old self out of the system, it is the only way to change. I wasn't the only one who had lived this way, who had built a life around control disguised as love, who had learned from childhood that survival meant adaptation, that affection was something you earned through performance, that trust was a currency that had to be carefully calculated,

Your New Self

given in just the right amount, but never too much. It was everywhere. It was in the way we are raised, the way we are taught to succeed, the way society itself functions, rewarding those who know how to play the game, who know how to say the right things, who know how to bend reality to their advantage, punishing those who are too raw, too honest, too open, too willing to love without strategy, without armor, without an exit plan. I began to see it in everything—in marketing campaigns designed to manipulate emotions, in relationships that were more about control than connection, in friendships that were built on unspoken hierarchies of power, in families that functioned on obligation rather than genuine love, in a world that encouraged competition over collaboration, self-interest over sincerity, presentation over truth.

For more than 20 years, I had been breathing in lies, and I didn't even know it. The heartbreak was no longer just about him. It was about everything. It was about the way I was conditioned to hide my true self in order to be accepted, to manipulate rather than express, to chase validation instead of connection, to build walls instead of bridges, to trade authenticity for power, to use love as a means to an end rather than an end in itself. And it was in that realization that something inside me finally began to shift. I didn't want to live like this anymore. I didn't want to keep wearing masks, keep playing roles, keep bending myself into whatever shape I thought would make people love me; I wanted to kill my old self.

Life in Saigon

In my late twenties, I encountered other important lessons about lies, about power, I graduated from university with a Bachelor in Human Resources Management and listened to my mother and moved back to Vietnam for a few years to live and work, living a life that seemed perfect. A high-paying job at a university, total independence, fancy restaurants, endless parties, and meeting successful entrepreneurs in Saigon's elite social circles. I had finally found what I lacked in my years in Canada- the illusion of status, beauty, exclusivity. The most glamorous clubs, the most expensive dinners, the most sought-after men. And I thought I had won.

By night, my friends and I ruled the city. We were young, beautiful, and ambitious. We walked into the most exclusive clubs and sat at tables where men showered us with champagne and luxury. We had everything—expensive condos, glamorous lifestyles, men who pursued us relentlessly. It was a constant chase. We measured our worth by the attention we received, by who got invited to the best tables, by who was dating the most powerful man in the room. I wore heavy makeup every time I stepped out, terrified of being seen without it. Every relationship lasted three months at most—there was always someone better, someone richer, someone more exciting.

During that time, I opened my own businesses—a milk tea store and an education company. Running these ventures was one of the most profound and humbling experiences of my life, a mirror reflecting back all the things I didn't know about myself. My ambition. My competitiveness. My hunger for success. My inability to trust. And most of all, my deep-seated control issues.

With my many years of experience in service industry in Canada, I had the skills and knowledge to scale these businesses quickly. Sales skyrocketed, productivity was at its peak, and customers became fiercely loyal. We launched new marketing campaigns, introduced fresh product lines, built hype, took photos with customers, and ensured our brand was everywhere. Within three weeks, I tripled our sales through sheer aggression—aggressive marketing, aggressive customer relationship-building, and aggressive employee management. Every customer who walked through our doors was treated like royalty.

My Story

Every employee was either a high performer or they were out. There was no space for mediocrity. No room for comfort. By month nine, we were able to expand to a second location. On paper, I was thriving. But in reality, this business wasn't just teaching me about money—it was exposing cracks in my foundation. I worked relentlessly, stressed about competitors stealing my recipes and connections, obsessed over micromanaging every detail to maintain control. I established a toxic and tense working environment, numbers were more important. What I failed to see was that while I had built a financially successful business, I had also created a toxic working environment where fear, pressure, and control ruled. In that system, I saw nothing more than revenue, expansion, domination. But the truth was, I had built something that looked strong on the outside but was fragile on the inside. And deep down, I was just as trapped emotionally and mentally.

I met a group of high-level entrepreneurs. Not just rich people—financially and politically powerful people. They weren't just running businesses; they were playing at the highest levels, managing multi-million-dollar investments, sitting at the intersection of politics and entrepreneurship. And for the first time, I lived in that extreme success world but the experience was totally unexpected.

All of them, managed more than 3 businesses each. One of them, my closest business partner, managing three businesses with over 5 projects at once, would work until 5 AM every night. He barely slept. His meals were rushed, often just fast food in plastic containers. His eyes were sharp, his mind was brilliant, but his energy was… empty.

No life. No soul. Just work.

I saw the private jets, the yachts, the designer suits—everything I once admired. But I also saw the exhaustion, the paranoia, the stress that never left their faces. They were always on edge, chasing more, cautious, suspicious, projecting, calculating the next moves. They were all trapped in the what-ifs and what-shoulds. They couldn't stop. They had investors to answer to, employees to pay, debts to cover. The empire they built owned them.

The business world was ruthless. No one cared how hard we worked, our plans, or our passion. It was cutthroat.

I was in it too—the chase.

My Story

The relentless, exhausting, soul-draining chase for numbers—more leads, more followers, more profit, more success—hitting sales targets, outpacing competitors, and making sure the charts kept climbing. And with it came the endless cycle of pressure, deception, and manipulation—strategies designed to grab attention, create demand, and push our brand forward at any cost.

And we did it. We tripled sales. We crushed KPIs. We generated leads and hit revenue targets.

But at what cost?

Along with those "wins" came something else, something that slowly drained the soul out of me. The yelling at the marketing team when their campaigns weren't brainwashing enough, when they didn't create the urgency, we needed to get people into buying. The cutthroat environment was where we pushed employees into impossible KPIs, where they worked themselves into exhaustion, and where they knew they were disposable if they didn't perform. The firing. The control. The endless competition.

All of it, in the name of growth. But grow in what was the question I asked myself.

Because in the business world, everything was capped. No matter how much we sold or scaled, it was just a machine that demanded more—more pressure, more exhaustion, more manipulation, more competition. That was all.

I had chased success with everything I had, and yet, standing in the middle of it, I felt empty.

At first, I told myself it was just part of the game. But soon, the game started playing me. I was constantly on edge, trapped in a loop of work that never truly ended. The weight of it was so heavy that I started feeling it physically—numbness creeping up my arms, coldness settling into my hands like my body was slowly shutting down. There were days I couldn't get out of bed, my head pounding with an unbearable ache, my mind overloaded to the point that even basic conversations became a struggle. I would talk to my cousin and catch myself saying absolute nonsense, my brain so scattered, so overworked that I was barely coherent. I had to be cautious in everything I said and did; there were many times I decided not to say what I truly wanted to express. The stress I had to take in at work crept out another way. I snapped at my family when they asked for my attention, their constant calls and concerns irritating me to my core, as if their love was an inconvenience rather than the thing keeping me tethered to reality. I became

My Story

a beast—reactive, impatient, angry, always on the verge of explosion. I wasn't myself anymore. I had no space to think, breathe, or even feel. Then one night, I reached for the bottle. Sleeping pills. Tylenol for the headache that never left.

And in that instant, everything stopped.

This was the moment. The moment I realized I was at my breaking point. Many of us out there—we don't even realize it. We don't see how the stress slowly creeps in, how the occasional Tylenol for a headache becomes a daily necessity, how sleeping pills start feeling like the only way to rest. We don't question it because we assume it's just life. The pressure, the exhaustion, the constant mental overload. It's just how things are, right?

I was lucky. Lucky because I had seen it before. I had watched my aunt fight depression for over a decade, relying on pills just to get through the day. I had seen my cousin struggle; my uncle drink himself into oblivion to escape the same weight. And I was on the same path, blindly walking toward the same numbness, the same quiet destruction.

How many of us are living like this? How many of us are one more sleepless night away from breaking? How many of us are so caught up in chasing success, validation, and security that we don't even realize we're sacrificing ourselves in the process?

We tell ourselves we're fine. We pop a pill. We push through.

My aunt's story flashes through my mind like an echo from the past, reminding me of something I had overlooked. She was ambitious, relentless, always working, always striving, but even she had moments to breathe. She had space, however limited, to sit with herself at night, to exist outside of the frantic chase for more. But these people—my business partners, the ultra-successful, the ones running billion-dollar ventures and jet-setting around the world—they have nothing but the chase. The life I always wanted, the one I thought had it all—power, wealth, prestige—is actually poor in ways I never considered before. Poor in emotional stability, in mental peace, in the quality of their lives. Obligations consume their entire existence, pressures, fears of failure, frantic thoughts, and predictions of what's to come next. There is no pause button. No peace. No freedom.

And suddenly, I see the cruel irony.

Poor people are trapped in survival.

Rich people are trapped in ambition.

Both are running. Both are exhausted. Both are poor in their own ways.

The Moment It Clicked

The second my hand touched that bottle, something inside me shifted. A deep, primal awareness woke up in me.

No. This is not the path.

I didn't need a doctor to tell me. I didn't need anyone to diagnose me. I knew. I knew I was on the wrong road, and if I didn't stop now—if I didn't take control—I would end up somewhere I never wanted to be—depression, tumor, death.

Wealth without Chains

As I told you earlier, I worked relentlessly for over a decade, from age 16 to 27. My life was built around *more*. More work, more money, more achievements, more security. I pushed myself beyond my limits, 12–16-hour workdays, day after day, year after year, driven by an invisible fear—the fear of not having enough, the fear of financial instability, the fear of an uncertain future. It consumed me. I did everything I thought I was supposed to do.

Your New Self

At 27 years old, I bought a million-dollar condo in Vancouver, a milestone that I was very proud of. Around the same time, I was diagnosed with spinal dysfunction. Everyone was surprised—this condition wasn't supposed to happen until much later in life. But chronic overwork had taken its toll. Years of stress, sitting for endless hours, neglecting my body, living only for the grind—had finally caught up with me.

My spinal cord became compressed, the bones in my back displaced, crushing the nerves that ran through them. The back pain was relentless—a dull, never-ending ache on my left side, and it followed me all the time.

I had sacrificed my health for wealth. I am sure many of us here are on the same boat.

During COVID, I moved back to Canada because my parents feared I'd get stuck in Vietnam—but what I walked into was nothing like the safety they hoped for. It was the strangest chapter of my life. Inflation hit like a silent storm; the economy was collapsing—I saw it all so clearly. Inflation soared. The world froze. Entire industries collapsed overnight. Groceries were even more expensive than the hourly wage people got, not including other bills. Then I learnt about how money was printed and credited. I realized the ugly truth: We are all playing

My Story

in a system controlled by people who understand money better than we do. And if we don't learn the game, we will always be trapped.

The world took a turn none of us expected.

The pandemic swept through, and suddenly—like everyone else—I was confined. Not just within the four walls of my home, but within the depths of my own mind. Stripped of the usual distractions of daily life and career pursuits, I faced an unsettling silence.

And in that silence, I finally saw the chaos I had buried within.

For the first time, there was nowhere to hide from my own thoughts—no external achievements to mask the turmoil I carried.

Sitting in isolation, I saw the world outside for what it was: still, unmoving, locked down, yet brimming with an intensity that had nothing to do with my imagined fears. Lives were being lost. Families were separated. Uncertainty hung over us all like a storm cloud.

My fears of judgment?

My anxiety about someone not liking me?

My worries about success or failure?

In that larger context, they became so small.

All around, the news was saturated with terrifying images: bodies on the streets, exhausted doctors and nurses overwhelmed by a relentless virus, empty shelves in stores, people fighting over the simplest supplies—fueled by a primal fear of scarcity, of extinction.

The world was in survival mode.

I was oceans away from my family, isolated in Canada, unable to protect them. My loved ones were dragged to testing centers, and if they tested positive, they'd be taken away to quarantine facilities. My grandmother, at eighty-five, and my aunt, at seventy-five, were at the greatest risk. Seniors didn't often come back once they were admitted to hospitals.

The very thought paralyzed me.

This invisible virus—so small it could only be seen under a microscope—had the power to bring humanity to its knees.

That's when I realized something profound:

My entire understanding of power was crumbling.

How could I be strong in this moment?

What did strength even mean in the face of something I couldn't see, let alone control?

I learned, in that helplessness, not to wish, not to hope—but to insist that my family would be safe. That

My Story

they were okay. I had only one choice: to command my mind to think differently. I had no power to physically protect them, but I could shield my mind from spiraling into fear.

My only option was to feed myself strong, positive thoughts—even if they were lies.

And in that forced shift, I discovered an unexpected strength.

In those moments of helplessness, I uncovered a strategy—

A true form of power: using lies to manipulate lies.

In this book, I won't just tell you my story—I'll help you discover your own.

I'll share the methods that gave me an unshakable foundation—approaches that brought freedom and resilience to my life, and which I believe can do the same for you. This is an invitation to a life of power, strength, and clarity.

I'm excited to share these tools with you, so you, too, can live with renewed power and purpose.

It's time to stop looking outside for solutions and start recognizing the extraordinary power you've had all along.

Your New Self

"You have power over your mind—not outside events. Realize this, and you will find strength."
—Marcus Aurelius

In that suffocating moment of quarantine, what felt like a complete disaster, a standstill in life—turned out to be the greatest turning point I never expected. It's where I discovered the secrets and methods to conquer the deepest sufferings that had silently shaped my life. It's where I found freedom from pain and clarity I never knew I needed.

Everything changed.

The notion of control, once something I thought I had, had vanished completely.

Also during this strange and quiet time, I uncovered the root of our financial chase—and the emotional suffering that always seems to follow it.

I looked a bit deeper into the current financial system. I devoured books—Think and Grow Rich, Rich Dad Poor Dad, The New Great Depression—and with every page, my understanding of money, success, and security began to shatter. I dove deep into macroeconomics, inflation, the history of money, Bitcoin, decentralized finance, stock investments, and wealth-building strategies. And what I discovered changed everything. The key is about how well you protect and grow what you already have. And in my journey of studying the macroeconomic landscape, here are some key ways that have helped me in becoming financially stronger.

Power of Financial Leverage in Real Estate

I learned one of the most important financial truths: Wealth is not about how hard you work. It's about how well you make money work for you. Financial leverage, when used in the right way, is one of the most powerful tools in wealth creation. We can use leverage for real estate investments but we need to use it with extreme caution. We should only buy properties where the rental income completely covered my mortgage payments, allowing us to build wealth while keeping my finances free from stress. Do not take reckless loans. Do not make impulsive decisions based on market hype. Every investment must calculate, precise, and backed by thorough observations and research. In fact, the real estate market offers endless opportunities, but they are only available to those who know where to look. There are high growth properties but in more affordable areas, we just need to seek hard enough, spend time around the area long enough and talk to the right people. Instead of guessing, we should follow those who are already successful in real estate, learning directly from them. Whenever we visit potential properties, we should bring these mentors along, absorbing their insights, their strategies, and their ability to spot real value.

Gold

Gold is not a man-made system—it is a gift from God, a natural reserve of wealth that no one can manipulate. That is why the wealthiest families, institutions, and governments always have gold in their portfolios. Gold is safe and valuable to invest in because it is a deep-rooted belief in wealth that spans generations. And this is impossible to replace. Gold is, in my view, one of the safest and most tangible asset classes. It boasts high liquidity, allowing for easy conversion into cash whenever needed, and the way it is stored offers unparalleled privacy, ensuring complete control and security over one's wealth.

Digital Assets

In a world where governments print trillions of dollars at will and the world evolves into a digital era,

My Story

digital assets like Bitcoin and Ethereum I view as digital assets built and grown by the younger generations. I'll be honest—when I first encountered cryptocurrencies, I was skeptical, I could not fully grasp the technology, the birth of it, or the mechanics behind how it functioned on a deep technical level. But despite my initial skepticism, I chose to invest and made very good profits from it. Overtime, I see the shift in the world, the emerging financial architecture, and the intellectual wealth of future generations being built on these assets.

The New Me

Also during this strange and quiet time, I uncovered the root of our financial chase—and the emotional suffering that always seems to follow it.

I have taken you through the evolution of a ridiculously wild and free-spirited child, to a teenager who slowly erased herself to fit into a world that did not understand her, to a woman in her late twenties chasing status, luxury, and a version of success that I thought would make me whole. And now, after all the searching, the breaking, the rebuilding—I have finally arrived at the most blissful and liberated version of myself. A version that no longer lives for the next moment. For the first time in my life, I feel enough. And it is the strangest, most unexpected revelation—the moment I stopped chasing more, I felt wealthier, freer, more secure, and more pumped about life than ever.

I realized that little five-year-old girl with her wild bird's nest hair, who once dreamed with such clarity, before the world told her what she should do. She dreamed of an ordinary and peaceful life. And now, after everything—after peeling back the layers of societal expectations and unlearning the 'musts' and 'shoulds,' freeing myself from the weight of judgments and anxieties—I see it so clearly. All along, my inner child knew the way. I don't need the biggest empire. I don't need the fanciest lifestyle. I don't need to be somewhere else. I just need the ordinary. A small business built with heart, a peaceful home filled with warmth, a neighborhood where kindness flows effortlessly, and a community that uplifts rather than competes. I want a life where I wake up each morning with ease, unburdened by the world's pressures, a life that is simple yet abundant, ordinary yet extraordinary in its own way. I want to live a life where success is measured not by numbers but by the depth of joy, the strength of connections, and the freedom to live on my own terms.

My Story

This simple, ordinary, joyful life is what I was looking for all along.

The Saigon I knew before wasn't the one I see now. Back then, I couldn't feel its pulse, rawness, or inspiration. I was too distracted by the noise, the chase, the illusion of what success was supposed to look like. I thought luxury was freedom, but at its purest form, it was rigid, exhausting, and boxed in. In the world I knew before, love came with conditions. It was cautious, skeptical, and calculated. Because when money, status, and expensive gifts were involved, life and connections became an exchange. Options diluted sincerity. Affection was measured. Trust was a gamble.

Instead of those late nights spent under neon lights in high-rise buildings, trapped behind a screen, chasing deadlines and numbers, I now wake up with the sunrise. I step outside just as the world is slowly stretching awake, when the air is still fresh and crisp, untouched by the chaos of the day. The birds sing songs that get drowned out by the noise later in the day. The trees release their morning scent before the smell of gas and concrete takes over. The city is softer, more vulnerable, as if it hasn't yet worn its armor. I see Uber drivers huddled around a tiny coffee stand, laughing over steaming cups with the owner before their long shifts. Street vendors are setting up their stalls, carefully arranging their goods with the same quiet pride and intention they do every morning. Store owners rolling up their metal doors, greeting the day with sleepy smiles, standing in their little pockets of the world they've built for themselves. These moments inject a quiet rush of love into my soul—a love for life and the smallest, most ordinary things.

Mornings used to feel like a race against time. The second I woke up, my mind was already flooded with a to-do list: emails to check, calls to make, deadlines to hit. My body moved on autopilot, rushing from task to task, inhaling breakfast like it was a chore, all while my eyes were glued to a screen.

Now, before work, I water my plants, letting my fingers brush against their leaves, feeling the freshness of the soil. I drink my coffee slowly, appreciating its warmth, the richness of the aroma, the way it feels as it moves through my body. I cook my own breakfast, taking the time to enjoy the rhythm of cooking—the chopping, the stirring, the sizzling of food hitting the pan. It's no longer about *fueling* my body just to function—it's about committing to *nourishing* myself first, physically and emotionally.

My Story

Something I never had time for before. Slowing down has improved my health, mood, and entire quality of life.

On weekends, I ride a simple bike through the city, the wind rushing against my skin, weaving through the streets easily. I feel free. I watch Uber scooter drivers move through dense traffic with a skill that is effortless and precise; it feels almost like art. They navigate between cars and motorbikes like water flowing through cracks, untouchable, independent, free. These riders know every shortcut, every hidden alley, every change in land prices before anyone else. They are connected to the city's pulse in a way most people never will be.

And everywhere I go, I give happily.

Every day, I tip generously, hand money to those who need it, share what I have freely—because I no longer grip onto it with fear. I release the need to hoard, to cling, to measure my worth by what I own. And for the first time, I feel truly alive. Ironically, even though I now make less and have less than I did before, I feel safer, more at peace, more abundant than ever.

I now have time for my loved ones, not just physically, but emotionally. I sit with them, listen to them, support them. I no longer react impulsively, no longer snap in frustration or feel the constant pressure of chasing something I can never catch. I am simply here, fully present. Whatever comes, comes, I will resolve whatever comes along the way. I connect more with my closest friends, sitting together for hours, sharing stories that matter, laughing until our stomachs hurt. I roam the streets indulging in street food, savoring flavors without rushing, without checking my phone for the next task. Some days, I hop on a bike and explore the city, or ride to my best friend's house, spending the afternoon with her and her mom, cherishing the simple, warm moments that money can never buy.

I now see life but in a different way—the beauty of it in its rawest, most ordinary form.

I am getting a farmland near Saigon, building a modern Zen house with a private creek, a sanctuary design with a small garden for organic veggies, where I can spend mornings tending to the earth, feeling grounded, letting nature be both my exercise and my meditation. I want my family to live closer to me, to build a space where we can all find solace and connection, away from the world's noise. Instead of chasing a penthouse in the city, why not trade it for a peaceful home in the countryside, with fresh air and space to breathe? Instead of buying overpriced organic vegetables, why not grow

My Story

them? Instead of feeling trapped in an exhausting cycle of "more," why not decide where "enough" is?

I am also bringing to life a small milk tea cart business, a tribute to Saigon's vibrant street culture and the childhood dream of a little girl who once imagined owning her own food stall. I envision it in one of the most iconic corners of the city, a place deeply woven into the cultural fabric of Saigon, where people gather, connect, and share moments over a simple yet comforting drink. This is not just a business—it is a piece of my past, a promise fulfilled to the fearless, imaginative child within me who once dreamed without limits. Now, I have decided to make it come true for her.

The four dimensions of my life—mental, emotional, physical, and financial stability—finally found their balance. I stopped being a prisoner to work, no longer spending endless hours in front of a screen, micromanaging every dollar, every opportunity, every possible outcome. Instead, I started living. I spend my time with clear intentions now, I spend time and money on things that make me feel alive rather than just "productive." I take long rides to the countryside, exploring lands and learning about their values—not because I need to make an urgent investment, but because I simply love it. I still enjoy wealth-building, but I no longer let it define me. It is part of my life, but it is no longer my lifeline.

Rewiring My Mind: The End of Manipulation

I thought wealth was the only path to freedom. I know many of you reading this might be thinking the same thing right now: How can I live well without chasing more? How can I feel safe without constantly striving for money? It's a question that traps so many of us for a lifetime—a question that convinces people to trade their peace, their values, and even their soul in exchange for a false sense of security. But that belief is the biggest lie we've been sold. And in this book, I'm going to show you exactly why—and how true power has nothing to do with how much you have, but everything to do with how we live. I will show you how to build a fearless life—step by step—by peeling back the layers of fakeness, conditioning, and silent pressure you have carried for years. Beneath it all lies the purest gift God gave you—your true essence. That's where your unique talent lives. Until you find that, happiness will always feel just out of reach, and success will never feel like enough. This book will guide you to uncover the real reasons behind your restlessness,

My Story

your anxiety, and the bone-deep exhaustion of trying to keep up in a world that never stops spinning.

In this book, I'm not here to sell you another formula for success—I'm here to hand you the secrets of how to achieve true power that I've painfully learned, so you don't have to waste many years like I did. I hope it helps you return to yourself—and helps us build a softer, more beautiful world, together.

I no longer manipulate, nor do I cling to outcomes. Each day, I make a conscious choice to act with awareness, to eliminate habits and behaviors that drain me or negatively impact those around me. I refuse to convince myself to stay in places, jobs, or relationships that don't align with my values. I no longer twist reality just to fit my comfort zone. Love was once a cycle of highs and lows, of fleeing when things got too hard, of chasing when things felt uncertain. Before, love was different. I acted not out of love, but out of personal benefit, out of need, out of the desire to gain something in return. And in doing so, love always went against me. It was a battle, a constant push and pull, a painful cycle of attachment and disappointment. I did not consciously choose to love—I only sought to receive it.

Now, love is a practice, a commitment, a willingness to sit with discomfort rather than escape it. In doing so, I have watched the quality of my life shift in profound ways. My relationships are deeper, my sense of self is stronger, and my well-being—both financial and emotional—feels more stable than ever. Love, in particular, has been redefined. For the first time in my life, I find myself on a journey of patience in love, something I never imagined I would be capable of.

I feel extremely grateful. When I am ready, the universe sends to my life someone who does not simply come and go, does not turn away when things get difficult, stays, even when I push away. He does not love me only in my best moments; he holds space for me in my worst. He challenges me, forces me to confront parts of myself I would rather ignore, and teaches me lessons that no book, financial success, or personal milestone ever could. When I agree to act with love, love comes to me. It flows naturally, effortlessly, like the rising sun that never questions its purpose—it simply shines.

The greatest blessings often arrive disguised as challenges. For the first time in my life, I am learning to stay—not out of fear, not out of obligation, but out of conscious choice. For the first time, I am not running

My Story

at the first sign of discomfort, not seeking escape when things become difficult, not allowing my old patterns of avoidance to dictate my actions. I am choosing to remain present, to allow myself to be challenged, questioned, and seen for who I truly am—flaws, complexities, and all. And love, in its truest form, is perhaps the greatest challenge of all. It strips away illusions, exposes the deepest vulnerabilities, and forces us to grow unexpectedly. We are imperfect, two flawed individuals navigating our own fears and uncertainties, but somehow, in this shared space of imperfection, I am able to explore the most profound, transformative, and deepest feelings of all.

For the first time, I understand that love is not just about the fleeting highs or the rush of excitement—it is about the quiet, unshakable decision to choose each other, over and over again. It is about facing the discomfort, embracing the growing pains, and finding a deeper joy in staying, committing, and loving with intention. And in that choice, I have discovered a kind of transformation I never thought possible—a love that doesn't just happen to me, but one that I actively create.

I am learning that love is not just about the beautiful moments—it is about the ugly ones too.

Your New Self

The late nights of silence when we don't know what to say, the fights that leave us exhausted and questioning, the miscommunications, the doubts, the moments where it feels easier to leave than to stay because now, I have the capacity to stay, and I treat love with a grateful heart.

Of course, it is not perfect. I am still learning daily, challenging myself, and pushing through the discomfort of growth. But that is what makes it beautiful—the learning, the testing, the falling, the trying again, the realization that love is not a destination but a journey. I am learning to forgive, trust, work through, and be kind in disappointments. I am learning to be more open, more vulnerable, to communicate even when the words feel heavy, even when the conversation feels impossible. I am learning patience—not just in waiting, but in sitting with discomfort, in holding space for both my emotions and someone else's, in resisting the impulse to shut down or run away.

I have realized love is the most powerful force because it breaks us open so we can become more. It forces us to sit with our imperfections, to embrace our fears, to stretch ourselves beyond what feels comfortable. It calls us to rise, to choose understanding over ego, to practice acceptance even when it is hard, to forgive even when I don't feel like it.

Love no longer feels like a chase or a battlefield. It becomes a force of expansion—a force that makes us softer, stronger, wiser. A force that teaches me that real love is not about winning or losing, nor is it about control. It is about choosing, every single day, to show up. To be present. To be seen and to see another. And in that choice, we have become something greater than we ever were alone.

Coming Home to Myself

After thirty years of searching, breaking, rebuilding, and transforming, I now stand before you with the deepest realization of all. That fearless little girl—the one who once dreamed without limits, who expressed without hesitation, who lived with untamed curiosity—never truly disappeared. She was buried beneath layers of expectations, fears, and conditioned beliefs. But she came back to combat.

She is not the same. The storms she once feared have reshaped, transformed, and refined her. She has walked through the fire, endured heartbreaks, betrayals, losses, and suffering, only to rise stronger. She has taken the purest form of who she once was and elevated it into her most powerful form.

That bird's nest hair kid

She won.

She overcame the timid, fearful, overthinking, artificial version of herself that life had tried to shape her into.

This is what it means to be the highest, most powerful version of ourselves in God's creation.

Preface

Unlike most books where authors express deep gratitude to their loved ones for unwavering support, my experience was quite the opposite. When I told my closest friends and family that I was writing a book, their reactions weren't filled with encouragement. Some laughed. Some were skeptical. Some didn't even acknowledge it.

"Do you even have enough knowledge to write a book and educate others?" one person asked.

"You have to be famous first. Then you can sell a book," another said.

I was surprised, but more than that, I was deeply grateful. Their words didn't discourage me—they fueled me. They ignited an even greater determination to publish this book and share it with the world. I believe

My Story

that every voice, every story, and every perspective hold immense value—not because of external validation, but because they are the most precious gifts that God has given us to make this life more beautiful. I believe life is a masterpiece, and each of us is a puzzle piece within it. Each of us carries something unique, something irreplaceable—our struggles, our triumphs, our lessons, and our perspectives. And whether we realize it or not, we are all contributing to something greater. Without our stories, the picture of life remains incomplete. Without our experiences, the world lacks depth.

We are all here trying to make sense of this life.

I don't want to live in a world where we all keep our struggles locked inside, pretending to be fine. I don't want to live in a world where we settle for mediocrity because chasing something bigger feels too uncertain, too risky.

So this book?

This is my way of contributing to the magic.

As Mahatma Gandhi once said:

"Be the change that you wish to see in the world."

And that is my goal—to be the change I wish to see in the world.

The change I dream of, it's the kind of world where each individual on this planet all gets access to the greatest power. Where people heal more, hurt less. Where children grow up in homes filled with love and emotional security. Where relationships are built on truth, not survival. Where ambition and success do not come at the cost of our mental and emotional well-being.

A world where, as Gary Chapman so beautifully put it:

> *"I dream of a day when the potential of married couples in this country can be unleashed for the good of humankind, when husbands and wives can live life with full emotional love tanks and reach out to accomplish their potential as individuals and as couples. I dream of a day when children can grow up in homes filled with love and security, where children's developing energies can be channeled to learning and serving rather than seeking the love they did not receive at home."*

If you and I were sitting across from each other right now—just the two of us, coffee in hand, in a quiet corner of the world—you'd probably recognize parts of your own story in mine. Because while the details may be

My Story

different—the places, the people, the choices—the *feelings*? The lessons? Those are universal.

When we share who we truly are—our raw, unfiltered truths—we create something far bigger than ourselves. And that is the most electrifying, euphoric feeling of all. Like an explosion of energy, an adrenaline rush, a dopamine high—from the stimulation of our minds breaking past old barriers, from the collision of perspectives, from the deep, exhilarating realization that we are not alone in our struggles, our dreams, our search for meaning. Like music—the way individual notes, on their own, might seem ordinary, but when they join together, they create a **symphony so breathtaking, so profound, that it moves the soul.** Like the ocean—where every single wave, no matter how small, merges into something vast, something unstoppable, something **majestic.**

And that is my goal, for us, to create that moment of connection, of expansion, of seeing something we have never seen before. It is the thrill of seeing the world in a new way together. It is the ecstasy of shattering old beliefs and stepping into something bigger, something deeper, something that shakes the very foundation of who we thought we were.

And so, I am here, writing these words, and you are here, reading them. That is no coincidence. Maybe you picked up this book for a reason. Maybe life has brought you to this exact moment, at this exact time, because there is something here that will resonate, something that will ignite a spark within you.

So let's begin, shall we?

1

Understanding the Inner Lies

Why Do We Have These Inner Lies (Negative Narratives)?

BECAUSE WE'RE HUMAN, and being human is a marvel of complexity—a living equation of instinct, emotion, memory, and survival. We are built from stories, from data, from generations of experience embedded into our very being. For years, that quiet question, *Why does it hurt so much to live?* Was answered by Billy Carson, a modern-day genius whose research on ancient civilizations, metaphysics, and human consciousness cracked something open inside me. He explained something I had never heard before: that our DNA isn't just biological code, it's a living archive—a storage system capable of holding up to 13.5 billion years of data. That means the grief, the heartbreak, the war, the fear of survival, our need for domination—all stored in our body. We're feeling echoes of every soul that came before us. And that realization, as shocking as it was, made everything finally make sense. In our essence, we hold both light and shadow—each designed to help us navigate life's challenges. This mix of strengths and vulnerabilities drives our need to survive, to shield ourselves. At its core, life can feel like a game, and manipulation often becomes an unspoken rule in this game. People manipulate not out of inherent malice, but because they've been subtly conditioned to believe that survival means controlling or rising above others. When we allow this shadow side to dominate, slipping into constant survival mode, the demon's voice appears. This is what happens when we let fear and insecurity steer the wheel, letting our lives fall out of balance. The demon's voice is the ego voice within us when our life is out of balance, it's the ego's whisper, craving validation, a sense of superiority, a fleeting control over circumstances and people. This craving manifests in countless forms—seeking attention, playing subtle mind games, or projecting carefully curated images—all in the pursuit of fame, wealth, and external validation.

It's essential to understand the origins of these lies because they're not random—they're layers of conditioning embedded in us over years. From a young age, we're surrounded by voices that shape our understanding of what's acceptable, what's "right," and what's achievable.

Understanding the Inner Lies

"You should have done this," "Don't ask that question," "Are you sure you can handle that?" "Only if you do this will you be successful." These statements, repeated over and over, embed themselves deeply in our minds, turning into beliefs that dictate our actions and self-worth.

Lies come from a place of fear. When people lie, it's often because they're trying to manipulate the outcomes by twisting the truth or hide something—whether it's to avoid discomfort, protect their image, or keep someone from getting hurt. We even have these so-called "white lies" that we tell to shield others from pain, but at the end of the day, a lie is a lie.

Over time, these external lies morph into internal ones. We start lying to ourselves as a way to justify our actions, making it easier to live with choices we're not proud of. Each lie sows seeds of inner distrust, feeding what I call the **"inner demon."** This inner demon—the accumulation of dishonest moments and ignored truths—begins to haunt us, not always in obvious ways, but subtly. This inner demon creates an atmosphere of fear and insecurity, shaping your beliefs and emotions in ways that can spiral.

Inner Lies and Emotional Pain

There are three core reasons behind the formation of Inner Lies, each of which plays a direct role in the emotional pain we experience. In this chapter, we'll peel back these layers to reveal the subtle habits and ingrained patterns that fuel this pain. Often, these patterns are so deeply embedded in our daily lives that, without intentional stillness and reflection, we miss their influence entirely. Here, I'll guide you in identifying these hidden triggers that contribute to the emotional distress you may be feeling right now. To truly dismantle an enemy, you must first understand its roots—how it forms, where it originates, and the specific actions, events, habits, and conditions that allow it to thrive in your life. This chapter will shine a light on those origins, helping you grasp why your Inner Lies take shape and why they manifest as emotional pain.

Root Causes of Emotional Pain

1. Suppressions: The Hidden Burden

Imagine your emotions are like the steam building up inside a rice cooker. At first, the cooker can handle it—there's just enough pressure to cook the rice perfectly.

Understanding the Inner Lies

But if you keep the lid tightly sealed, refusing to let any steam escape, that pressure doesn't just vanish. It builds, intensifies, and eventually, if left unchecked, it will force its way out, possibly spilling over and making a mess.

Emotions need to flow. But too often, we try to dam them up, pushing them down with distractions pretending they're not there.

Example:

Think of *Tom*, an energetic guy who seems to have it all together. But after a messy breakup, things start to change. He doesn't want to deal with the sadness or frustration, so he fills his days with distractions. He works late, hits the gym harder than ever, and goes out with friends every weekend. To everyone around him, it looks like he's "coping" just fine (Inner Lies).

But underneath that busy schedule, Tom is drowning. His avoidance of the emotions piling up is starting to affect him in ways he can't quite put his finger on. He snaps at friends over minor things, he's exhausted all the time, and, despite all the "fun" he's having, he feels completely disconnected. What started as emotional suppression is now turning into a deeper feeling of emptiness, and his body is starting to protest, too—constant headaches, tight shoulders, restless nights.

Tom thinks he's controlling the situation by staying busy. In his mind, as long as he doesn't stop moving, the pain can't catch him. But here's the kicker: **emotional pain doesn't vanish just because you ignore it. It gets stored away, building pressure until it leaks into every aspect of your life.**

You might not break down and cry in public, but the pain shows up in other ways. You start to feel more irritable, restless, or disconnected from things you used to enjoy. Your body might even react—tight muscles, frequent colds, or chronic fatigue. That's your unexpressed emotions talking.

Suppressing emotions is like leaving a garbage bag in your room for days until it starts to get rotten and smell. Its smell will start sneaking out of the room and other people can smell it. Our pain and negativity are like this garbage bag, the smell is your behavior when you are in pain. If you don't throw it out, it will influence your behavior, decisions, and health.

Tom's case isn't unique. Many of us have been there. We fill our calendars to avoid facing what's really going on inside (Inner Lies). But when we push our emotions aside, they don't disappear—they simmer below the surface, waiting for a moment of weakness to erupt.

2. Assumptions: The Trap of Others' Opinions

Emotional pain often sneaks up on us, **not from what actually happens, but from what we *think* is happening.** A huge source of this pain is from assumptions—specifically, the stories we make up in our heads about what others think of us (Inner Lies).

Example:

Let's talk about *Linh*, a gifted designer with a sharp eye for detail. Her work is admired, yet she's haunted by self-doubt. Whenever she sends a design draft to a client, she finds herself checking her inbox obsessively. If there's no reply within the hour, her mind jumps into overdrive: "*They probably hate it,*" "*I've messed this up,*" or "*I knew I wasn't good enough for this job*" (Inner Lies).

Her anxiety escalates, and soon, her mood shifts. She stops pitching bold ideas in meetings and avoids coffee breaks with her colleagues, believing they're silently judging her. But here's the truth: the client was just busy, and her colleagues weren't thinking about her at all—they were too wrapped up in their own deadlines. The stories Linh told herself were pure fiction.

Assumptions act like smoke—they cloud your vision and make things seem worse than they are. We convince ourselves that others are thinking negatively about us (Inner Lies), but in truth, most people are too focused on their own lives to give us as much thought as we imagine. The more we assume, the more we pull ourselves into a spiral of worry, which in turn shapes how we behave—often in ways that *create* the very outcomes we fear.

For Linh, it wasn't the client's delayed email that was the problem. It was the assumptions she made about it. The mind has a strange way of filling in blanks with worst-case scenarios. We think we're protecting ourselves by preparing for the worst, but instead, we're imprisoning ourselves in unnecessary unreal stories.

When you assume the worst, you act in line with those assumptions. If you believe people are judging you, you may shrink back, speak less, avoid opportunities, or isolate yourself. Over time, these behaviors create a self-fulfilling prophecy. You become less visible, and people engage with you less—not because they're judging you, but because you're distancing yourself.

3. Dishonesty: The Poison

People lie. We hear lies, we see lies, and eventually, we tell lies ourselves. As children, honesty was natural to us—we spoke without filters or fear. But as we grew up, we were introduced to a world where truth often took a backseat. Remember the shock and disappointment of encountering lies for the first time? Or the thrill of realizing that bending the truth could sometimes help us avoid consequences? Over time, dishonesty became something we learned, adopted, and, for many of us, even relied on.

Dishonesty is the act of being untruthful, deceitful, or intentionally misleading—not just in grand schemes but even in the smallest thoughts, words, or actions. It's not always about malicious manipulation; often, it disguises itself as harmless white lies, well-meaning half-truths, or convenient omissions. And that's precisely why dishonesty is so dangerous—it's vague, slippery, and easily rationalized. Most people associate dishonesty with deceit on a grand scale, but few consider the subtler forms, like a "necessary" lie to spare someone's feelings or a tweak of the truth to fit a narrative. Yet, as the very definition of dishonesty tells us, any deviation from the truth is an act of being untruthful.

Dishonesty comes in various forms, often serving different intentions. Some lies are intentional, while others arise from societal conditioning. For instance, *white lies* are often told with good intentions, aiming to protect someone's feelings. But hiding the truth—even with the intent to shield someone—still qualifies as a form of dishonesty. Then there are *embellishments*, when people alter or stretch the truth slightly, creating an illusion that eventually distances us from reality. Dishonesty can also stem from deeply ingrained societal beliefs, absorbed without question.

Take, for example, the unrealistic portrayals of relationships in movies, which paint love as effortless and flawless, setting up expectations that rarely match reality. Or, consider a child repeatedly told by a parent, *"You're not good enough."* These narratives, fed over time, shape perceptions and reinforce untrue ideas. Lies, at their core, distract us, cover up truths, or redirect attention. Each one, in its way, creates a dishonest reality that erodes authenticity.

It surrounds us in subtle, everyday ways—through exaggerated movie scenes, the unreal and shocking news on social media, or even the small, hidden truths in people around us. Over time, we absorb these distortions,

Understanding the Inner Lies

letting them quietly reshape our beliefs and how we see ourselves. This dishonesty is like a slow-acting poison, eroding trust and planting seeds of insecurity, building emotional walls that distance us not only from others but from our own true selves.

Here's the trap: dishonesty is often cloaked in justification. Whether it's to protect someone's feelings, avoid conflict, or gain an advantage, we rarely stop to question it. Instead, we defend it with phrases like, *"It's for their own good,"* or *"It's just a little lie."* But even the smallest twists of the truth leave an imprint on our soul, often unnoticed at first. The cost of dishonesty isn't paid upfront—it accrues slowly, wearing down our emotional integrity like water eroding stone. Over time, it creates a heaviness within us, a weight we may not even realize we're carrying.

Yes, dishonesty offers the illusion of convenience or the comfort of privacy. It feels like a quick fix. But in reality, lies are like bricks in a wall we build between ourselves and the truth. Over time, this wall becomes so high that we lose sight of what's real. Repeated lies create an alternate reality, one that is exhausting to maintain. Each lie demands another to support it, forming a tangled web that traps us in stress and self-doubt. It's not just our minds that suffer—our emotional health takes a hit too.

The constant need to uphold these fabricated narratives breeds mistrust and defensiveness, not just with others, but within ourselves.

Dishonesty leads to some of the deepest emotional pain because it's so easily rationalized, so deeply ingrained in how we navigate life. People interpret dishonesty differently, often defending their actions or downplaying the consequences without recognizing the true damage being done. What starts as a seemingly harmless lie eventually morphs into something far more destructive.

Example:

Emma and Lucas had been together for five years, sharing laughter, dreams, and a home. Their relationship seemed like the kind people admired—steady and loving on the surface. But over time, Emma noticed that Lucas had become more guarded with his phone. He'd tilt the screen away when she was nearby, excuse himself for "work calls," and become irritable when she asked innocent questions.

One evening, while Lucas was in the shower, Emma's curiosity got the better of her. She opened his phone and found a string of messages with a female colleague. Nothing overtly romantic, but there was a flirtatious undertone. She froze, her heart pounding. Instead of confronting him immediately, Emma decided to wait. She rationalized, *maybe it's harmless banter. Maybe I'm overreacting.* But deep down, she felt the sting of betrayal.

Lucas, on the other hand, knew he'd crossed a line. He told himself the messages were innocent, that they didn't mean anything. But the guilt started to eat at him. He became overly attentive to Emma, trying to make up for the dishonesty without admitting it. He'd bring her flowers out of the blue, plan surprise dinners, but Emma could sense something was off. His efforts felt forced, not genuine. The unspoken truth created a silent tension between them.

Over time, their once vibrant connection grew strained. Emma couldn't shake the feeling that Lucas was hiding something, and Lucas couldn't bring himself to confess. They started arguing over trivial matters, each deflecting their deeper issues. Lucas was caught in the exhausting loop of maintaining the lie, while Emma, unsure of what was real, began doubting her own worth.

The cost of dishonesty in their relationship wasn't just the immediate hurt—it was the slow erosion of trust, the emotional distance that grew between them. Lucas's unwillingness to be truthful and Emma's silence in the face of her suspicions created a divide neither could bridge. Their love, once full of joy and intimacy, became a hollow shell filled with resentment, insecurity, and unspoken words.

This example shows how dishonesty, even when it seems small or "harmless," can poison the foundation of a relationship. It's not just the act of lying; it's the ripple effect—the way it alters how we see ourselves, our partner, and the relationship. Emma and Lucas's story is a reminder that honesty, though uncomfortable at times, is the only path to true connection and healing. Without it, love becomes a fragile illusion, ready to shatter at the slightest touch.

As you move forward, note this: you are the author of your own story. These saboteurs may have shaped your past, but they don't have to dictate your future. By addressing them with courage and intention, you unlock the power to live authentically, love deeply, and thrive in alignment with your true self.

The next chapter will guide you deeper into dismantling these Inner Lies, equipping you with practical tools to unwire the pain circuit, turn these silent saboteurs into stepping stones for growth. Let's continue this journey together—toward the life of clarity, purpose, and emotional strength.

2

Unwiring the Pain Circuit

WHEN WE EXPERIENCE emotional pain, particularly after a significant life event like a breakup, loss, or betrayal, it often feels like we're trapped in a relentless loop of reliving the past. The memories cling tightly to our emotions, making it seem impossible to break free. After a breakup, for instance, every waking moment can feel like a battle just to get out of bed. The weight of shame, frustration, and hopelessness can overwhelm your heart, flooding your thoughts and making even the smallest tasks feel monumental.

Those memories, once beautiful, become tainted with pain. And that's where the struggle lies—not knowing how to release them. You find yourself searching for ways to erase what once brought joy but now only brings sorrow. The more you hold onto them, the deeper the emotional scars run. **Letting go isn't easy, because those memories are tied to the love and meaning you once**

held dear, making it feel as though moving forward means leaving behind a part of yourself.

It's human to try and fix what went wrong, to ask "what if," or to fantasize about a different outcome. We often become stuck in these moments because they are attached to love, joy, and experiences that were once meaningful. For many of us, memories represent something we wish we could relive or change, but the harder we hold on, the more trapped we feel.

Before the real enlightenment happened for me, I read countless books that explained techniques to "erase" or move past memories, but I remained stuck in darkness. The truth is, our bodies and minds are deeply connected to our memories. When we experience something painful, it's not just mental—it's physical. Our five senses are involved in creating those memories: the sound of a loved one's voice, the touch of their hand, the scent they wore. These sensory experiences create a powerful emotional attachment to the past.

Understanding the body-mind connection was a turning point for me. One day, I came across a teaching from Indian mystic Sadhguru, who explained that our bodies are masses of energy that perceive life through our senses. Our memories are the accumulation of sensory experiences, especially with people we've loved. When we hold onto these memories, it's because our emotions are tied to the sensations we felt with them.

One of the most important truths to understand about unwinding the pain circuit is this: **you need to give yourself time.** Healing isn't something you can rush or force; it's a process that requires patience and self-compassion. I can share with you the most powerful techniques in the world, but they will only work if you allow both your mind and your body the time they need to process, release, and heal. It's not just about letting go of painful memories in your mind—it's about giving your body the space to release the sensations and emotions tied to those memories.

If you try to rush this process, you'll fall into the same traps we talked about earlier—the roots of emotional pain that stem from suppression, assumptions, and dishonesty. Seeking a quick fix might feel tempting, but it leads only to greater suffering for you and for your loved ones. Turning to substances to numb the pain, burying yourself in distractions, or pretending the hurt doesn't exist won't heal you. Instead, these approaches will anchor the pain even deeper, creating a cycle that feels impossible to escape.

But here's the good news: there's a way out—a way that respects your journey and offers true, lasting liberation. The key is to honor your healing process, to give yourself the time and space to recover. Are you ready? Let's begin.

Build Your Fortress

The first step is to wield the power to manipulate lies and use them to dismantle your Inner Lies. To achieve this goal, you need to do one crucial thing: **gather strength and create the necessary space to heal from pain the *right way.*** Imagine your mind and soul as your body's immune system. When a virus invades, your body weakens. Without proper rest and care, the virus takes over. It's the same with emotional pain. After a breakup, a loss, or even a small disappointment, the sadness seeps in like a virus. Left unchecked, it invades every corner of your being, consuming your energy and leaving you paralyzed.

This is why creating a strong emotional immune system is vital. Without it, you can't effectively fight off the lies that creep in and sabotage you.

Let me paint you a picture: think of going into battle. Would you march onto the battlefield without weapons, without rest, or without a strategy? Of course not. You'd be an easy target. In the same way, when confronting your Inner Lies—your most cunning and relentless enemy—you need to arm yourself with strength and clarity. This inner demon isn't like an external opponent you can avoid or escape. It's closer, more intimate, and infinitely more dangerous. It's inside your own body, eventually sabotaging your life. This inner demon is like a trusted ally who betrays you. Isn't the sting of betrayal from a loved one far more painful than an attack from a stranger? That's what your Inner Lies do—they pretend to protect you while slowly eroding your soul. But here's the twist: this betrayal comes from *you*. It's your own mind turning against you.

To construct the unshakable foundation that shields you from emotional pain, there are five things you must seek in your life to be able to build this foundation for your life. These aren't quick fixes or surface-level solutions—they are profound, life-altering principles. When committed to, they won't just change how you respond to pain; they will redefine how you experience life. But here's the thing: they're not glamorous. They won't give you instant results or dramatic moments of epiphany.

They're repetitive, often mundane, and yes, sometimes tedious.

But that's the beauty of true transformation. Think of the lotus. Buried deep in the mud, its journey begins in complete darkness. For days, weeks, and even months, it fights through murky waters, unseen by the world. Its progress is slow and painstaking, layer by layer, inch by inch. From the surface, it seems as though nothing is happening. But beneath the water, the lotus is gathering strength, its roots anchoring deeper into the earth, preparing for something extraordinary.

And then, one day, it rises. It pierces the water's surface and blooms into a radiant flower—untouched by the mud it came from, untainted by the journey it endured. This is the essence of emotional transformation. The process is invisible at first, frustratingly slow, and often lonely. But every small action, every repetitive effort, builds resilience and strength beneath the surface.

Keep showing up, even when the progress feels invisible. Keep pushing, even when it feels dull or unimportant. Because, like the lotus, your breakthrough will come. And when it does, it won't be quiet or subtle. You'll feel it as a lightness in your chest, a clarity in your thoughts, and an unshakable calm that no external chaos can touch.

This is the power of mastering the mundane and trusting the process. As long as you're doing the right things, even the smallest actions are reshaping your life. Let's dive into the five principles that will nurture this transformation and help you rise to your own moment of radiance.

1. Seek Mother Nature

When you walk in nature and take a deep breath, each breath is an exchange—a release of tension, worry, and emotional baggage, and a welcoming of fresh, pure energy from the earth. The earth beneath your feet is ancient, wise, and limitless. It can absorb what you release without effort, without strain. That's why, after being surrounded by nature's energy, you feel more centered and calm. It's not just the act of being in a peaceful environment—it's an energetic exchange. **Mother Nature is there, holding you, protecting you, and reminding you that nothing is too heavy for her to bear.** The earth beneath your feet, the trees above, the air around you—they're all part of a powerful, nurturing force that can heal your soul. She's taking in what you no longer need, and in return, she gives you peace. The air you breathe, the ground you walk on, the trees that sway above you—they're all part of this healing process.

When you walk in the forest, observe the trees. They don't clamor for attention, yet their presence is undeniable. They're not trying to prove their worth or control their surroundings—they exist with quiet strength, deeply rooted in the earth, trusting the natural rhythm of life. It's humbling. In that moment, you realize how small your worries truly are in the grand scheme of things. Nature teaches us that we are just a part of a much larger, beautiful system, and that life will unfold as it is meant to, with or without our constant attempts to control it.

When we stay still and observe, nature shows us it operates under the natural law—a law that requires no force, no rush, no control. **It just *is*.** It simply allows. This is what makes nature so grounding—it shows us how to live in harmony with life's inevitable flow.

Think of the natural cycles: the sun rises, it sets, and the day moves on. The tree sheds its leaves in autumn, knowing new growth will come. Nature doesn't cling to any moment, and it doesn't mourn the past. It accepts the flow of life without question. When we immerse ourselves in nature, we start to adopt that mindset. We see that

Unwiring the Pain Circuit

nothing is permanent, that everything—our pain, our memories, our struggles—will pass. **The natural world reminds us that we are always in a state of becoming, always growing, always evolving.**

A powerful example of how spending time in nature can help heal and detach emotions from negative memories comes from the life of **Cheryl Strayed**, the author of *Wild: From Lost to Found on the Pacific Crest Trail*. Cheryl's journey into the wilderness is a real-life testament to the healing power of nature.

After the devastating loss of her mother and the subsequent unraveling of her life through grief, addiction, and the collapse of her marriage, Cheryl found herself overwhelmed by emotional pain. She felt trapped by the weight of her memories, unable to move forward. In a moment of desperation, she made a bold decision to hike over 1,000 miles of the Pacific Crest Trail, despite having no prior backpacking experience.

During her time on the trail, Cheryl experienced the raw beauty and solitude of the wilderness. The long stretches of hiking through forests, mountains, and deserts helped her disconnect from the painful memories that had dominated her life. Nature, with its vastness and simplicity, gave her the space to reflect, grieve, and ultimately release the emotional baggage she had been carrying.

As she walked day after day, surrounded by the natural world, Cheryl began to heal. The physical challenges of the trail—blisters, exhaustion, harsh weather—demanded her full attention, pulling her away from the cycle of overthinking and emotional pain. The trail taught her to focus on the present moment, to take each step as it came, and to embrace the peace that nature offered. By the end of her journey, Cheryl found a sense of clarity and emotional freedom she hadn't known before.

Her memoir, *Wild*, captures this transformative experience and has inspired countless people to turn to nature as a way to heal from emotional wounds. Cheryl Strayed's story shows that sometimes, it's in the vast, quiet spaces of the wilderness where we can finally let go of the past and find the strength to move forward.

Next time you find yourself overwhelmed by past memories or trapped in emotional pain, step outside. Let Mother Nature heal you. Spend just fifteen minutes watching the trees, feeling the earth beneath your feet, listening to the birds sing without a care in the world. Let the stillness and majesty of nature show you that life doesn't have to be so complicated. The natural law is always in effect, reminding us that in letting go, in trusting the flow of life, we find healing. Nature erases the noise, quiets the chaos, and brings us back to the truth—that everything will be okay, because it always has been.

2. Seek Silence

It's common that after a painful experience, our instinct is usually to either run from the pain or drown in it. We try to numb the hurt by keeping ourselves busy, or we get stuck replaying the memories, dragging ourselves through emotional mud over and over again. After Mother Nature has grounded us, her steady presence calming the storms within, we've created a safe space for our soul to begin trusting again. This is the foundation we need—but now comes the next step: **isolation into silence.**

Why silence? Because the Inner Lies that have embedded themselves within us are not our own. They've been absorbed, whispered, or even shouted into our minds by the toxic sources around us. The voices of judgment, comparison, and negativity don't originate from your soul—they're echoes of the outside world. And until you step away from the noise, you cannot separate what is truly yours from what was planted there by others. In silence, it isn't empty. It's full of answers. In the quiet, you'll hear the whispers of your intuition, the steady pulse of your heart, and the unfiltered truth of your soul.

In addition, it's not just about quieting the noise around you, but about taming the chaos within. After a painful experience, our minds become battlegrounds for emotions—anger, regret, sadness, anxiety, all swirling around and keeping us stuck in that negative space. These negative emotions, we often try to run from them, numb them, or overanalyze them. Even just fifteen minutes of silence gives you the space to **simply *be* with your emotions**. When you sit in silence, you are giving your brain permission to detox, breathe, and reset.

Think of your mind like a computer—when it's overloaded with too many open tabs (your thoughts and emotions), it starts to slow down, freeze, and eventually crash. Silence allows you to close those tabs one by one. It's a mental decluttering process that helps you sort through what's important and what's just emotional noise. And once the mind is clear, you can see the situation with new eyes, often realizing that the emotional weight you've been carrying isn't as heavy as it first seemed.

Mahatma Gandhi, a name synonymous with resilience and transformation, knew something many of us

Unwiring the Pain Circuit

forget in the noise of daily life: silence holds immense power. While leading an entire nation toward independence, Gandhi faced chaos, criticism, and pressure on an unimaginable scale. Yet, amidst the storm, he discovered his greatest strength—not in words or protests, but in silence.

Every Monday, Gandhi practiced a vow of silence, known as "maun vrat." On these days, he would not speak a single word. This wasn't about avoiding confrontation or escaping responsibility; it was about grounding himself. For Gandhi, silence wasn't an absence—it was a space for clarity, a way to confront the noise within. He believed that silence could cut through doubt and reveal the truth.

One of the most powerful moments of his life came during the planning of the Salt March in 1930, a pivotal act of civil disobedience that would inspire millions. At that time, Gandhi was surrounded by conflicting advice, political debates, and the expectations of an entire nation. He stepped away from it all, retreating into silence. While others demanded immediate action, Gandhi spent days in reflection, letting the answers emerge not from panic, but from peace. When he finally broke his silence, his path was clear, and the Salt March became a turning point in the fight for India's independence.

Silence, for Gandhi, wasn't a luxury—it was a necessity. It wasn't just about finding answers; it was about restoring his strength and connection to his higher purpose. He often said, "Silence is a great help to a seeker after truth." And truth, for Gandhi, was the foundation of everything—his decisions, his movements, and his ability to inspire millions.

What's even more extraordinary is how Gandhi's silence influenced those around him. It wasn't just his actions or speeches that moved people; it was his presence. His ability to remain calm under immense pressure became a beacon of strength for others. His silence wasn't passive—it was transformative, both for himself and for those who followed him.

When we allow ourselves moments of silence, we reconnect with our inner power. And from that space of stillness, we can move forward—not with haste, but with purpose. Gandhi didn't just fight for freedom, he lived it, and his silence was one of his greatest weapons.

3. Seek Inner Truth

Seeking Inner Truth is about uncovering the core of who you are—your desires, your needs, your mission, and your purpose in life. It's the deepest truth that belongs to you and only you. No one else can define it, find it, or even influence it because **it is uniquely yours.**

Too often, in moments of frustration, distress, or confusion, people instinctively look outward. They seek advice from others, distract themselves with conversations, or lose themselves in movies and social media. **This approach only adds noise to the chaos.** Other people's opinions are not your truth—they are reflections of their own experiences, values, and beliefs. Turning outward in such moments only makes you more confused and disconnected because those external voices drown out your inner voice.

Your Inner Truth is the key to your being. It holds the answers to why you wake up every day, why you were born, and what you are meant to do.

When you know your Inner Truth, nothing and no one can take you down mentally or emotionally and dim your light. It shields you from the toxicity of comparison, judgment, and doubt because you are anchored in what is most essential to you. But when you uncover your Inner Truth, you gain access to the strongest form of power of all.

Let me take you deeper into the power of silence and inner truth by sharing a story that embodies its transformative strength. Imagine someone like Alicia Keys, a world-renowned singer, who at the height of her fame, decided to take a step back—not because she was burnt out, but because she was haunted by the pressure to be perfect. From a young age, Alicia was told how to look, how to sound, and how to behave. The constant scrutiny from the media, the expectations from fans, and the relentless demand to fit into a mold began to take a toll on her soul. Despite her success, deep down she felt lost, disconnected from her true self, burdened by the weight of who she was supposed to be, rather than who she actually was.

Alicia's turning point came when she embraced silence, an act of rebellion against the noise of the world and her own inner critic. She would spend time in solitude, without makeup, without distractions, just sitting in stillness—reconnecting with the girl she had buried beneath years of a public persona. In that silence, she started to confront the painful memories that had shaped her: the pressures of growing up in the spotlight, the judgment, the self-doubt.

Through these moments of quiet reflection, Alicia realized that the version of herself that had been built by others was not her true identity. She began to release those past expectations, the need for validation, the emotional baggage of always striving to be someone else's idea of perfect. And as she sat in silence, she erased the past narratives that no longer served her.

When she emerged from this period of reflection, Alicia embraced a new chapter, one defined by self-love and authenticity. Her decision to go makeup-free in public wasn't just a statement about beauty—it was a declaration of self-acceptance, an act of erasing the old emotions tied to societal standards and embracing who she truly was. The past no longer held power over her, because she had reclaimed her identity in the quiet spaces of her mind.

This is why silence and Inner Truth are so powerful—they allow you to strip away the layers of expectations, pain, and false narratives that have weighed you down for years. By sitting with yourself, you give your mind and heart the space to release those old memories and emotional patterns, clearing the way for a new, unburdened version of yourself to emerge. Just as Alicia Keys erased the past pressures to conform, you too can erase the emotional ties that no longer serve you and begin living authentically, free from the shadows of the past.

This is a rebirth. Inner truth, **it gives you the gift of hearing your own voice again, unfiltered and true.** That's where real transformation begins.

4. Seek Reset (unlearning and rewiring)

A major reason people remain trapped in painful memories is that they assume the present and future will mirror the past. As author Wayne Dyer said, *"The past is a trail you leave behind, much like the wake of a speedboat. It has no power in the present unless you convince yourself that it does."*

When we wake up each day, we often repeat the same actions, interact with the same people, and follow the same routines. These habits become ingrained, and eventually, we operate on autopilot. But just as we learn habits, we can unlearn them.

This is the heart of your transformation—the moment where the old you begins to crumble, making space for the new. It starts with facing the raw, unfiltered truths about yourself—the ones you've avoided, the ones that sting, the ones that make you feel vulnerable, small, or even ashamed. But let me tell you, this isn't a punishment. It's the gateway to something extraordinary.

Resetting your life means questioning everything you thought you knew. It means humbling yourself to accept that what you've learned—what you've relied on—might not be the ultimate truth. It requires stepping into the unknown, relinquishing control, and feeling momentarily ungrounded. Yes, you'll feel off-balance. Yes, you'll feel foolish, perhaps even embarrassed. But this discomfort is necessary—it's the storm that clears the way for brighter skies. Just like bitter medicine cures a stubborn illness, this bitter process will cleanse your mind and soul. It's not easy, and it's not supposed to be. Growth never comes from comfort. The more you embrace this challenge, the greater your transformation will be. The old saying holds true here: "No pain, no gain." And let me assure you, the pain of this practice is temporary, but the power it unlocks within you is forever.

This concept may seem challenging to grasp, so let me break it down for you in a way that resonates deeply. Imagine you make a bold decision: from this moment forward, you commit to practicing absolute honesty. You vow to align every word you say with the truth. But inevitably, there will be days when old habits creep back in—moments when you catch yourself bending the truth, hiding something, or telling a small lie.

Here's the critical part: instead of beating yourself up, take a deep breath and say, *"It's okay. I forgive myself for this moment, and I'll do better next time."* This act of self-forgiveness is more powerful than you might realize. Each time you forgive yourself and recommit, you're doing more than just patching a mistake—you're unlearning the behaviors that no longer serve you. You're rewiring your brain, reshaping your identity, and rewriting your story in real-time.

Think of unlearning as shedding an old skin. By forgiving yourself, you're creating space for a new way of being to emerge. You're telling your brain, *"This is who I am now,"* and over time, this practice becomes a part of your essence. With repetition, honesty will embed itself so deeply into your character that lying will feel unbearable—like wearing shoes that don't fit. You'll have trained your brain to associate dishonesty with discomfort and integrity with alignment.

This transformation doesn't happen overnight, but with each small, deliberate step, you're crafting a new reality. Honesty won't just be something you *practice*—it will become who you are. And when that moment comes,

Unwiring the Pain Circuit

you'll feel a profound sense of freedom, knowing you've reclaimed control over your narrative and reshaped your life from the inside out.

Another example is when you practice letting go of your ego, you need to constantly remind yourself of humbling thoughts. Tell yourself things like, *"I don't know everything,"* or, *"Maybe they're partially right—how can I grow from this?"* These are the mental dialogues you must engage in daily to keep yourself grounded, to stop reacting out of pride, and to fight off that inner critic.

This process of unlearning is not a one-time event—it's an ongoing evolution. With each practice, you begin to see the world through fresh lenses, breaking free from the mental chains that have held you back. It's a journey of constant renewal, where your mindset evolves, layer by layer.

Unlearning is how you erase the weight of negative emotions and release the grip of past memories. It's the act of giving yourself permission to hit reset—to start at zero, to become a baby observing the world and embrace new thoughts, perspectives, and truths. Each time you allow yourself to adopt this beginner's mindset, you transform the very wiring of your brain.

Think of it as sculpting your identity. As you reshape how you perceive situations, your emotional responses naturally shift. Over time, this rewiring creates a new, grounded version of yourself—one that is not tethered to the pain of the past but rooted firmly in clarity, confidence, and authenticity. **This is the power of unlearning: it doesn't just change your thoughts; it changes *you*.**

One powerful way to practice unlearning and rewiring your emotional state is to write a letter to your past self. This seemingly simple act pushes you to step outside your current perspective, confront your truths, and observe your thoughts with raw honesty. It's a process that forces you to witness your pain, accept it, and begin the healing journey.

This notion of seeking your **Inner Truth** is the cornerstone of building an unshakable fortress within you. This process isn't just helpful—it's one of the most critical actions you must take for your life. Without it, you'll find yourself caught in a loop of doubt, fear, and confusion again. It's not something to rush or gloss over; it demands your full attention and dedication. That's why I want to take you through it step by step, with clarity and precision, so you can do it properly and effectively.

Unwiring the Pain Circuit

Let me take you to one of the darkest times in my life—after a painful breakup. I felt like my entire world had shattered. I was overwhelmed by guilt, shame, and bitterness, unable to escape the endless loop of "What if?" and "Why me?"

Here's what happened: I destroyed the relationship with my own stubbornness and egotistical behavior. It was toxic—on both sides. And one day after a fight, I saw him with another girl on the street, and that image tore through me like a dagger. It wasn't just heartbreak—it was humiliation. I'd always thought so highly of myself, believing I could charm anyone, even men in relationships. And now? I was the one cheated on. He didn't chase after me. He didn't even ask for forgiveness. I spiraled. My self-esteem didn't just hit rock bottom; it plummeted into the negatives. I couldn't face the world. For three months, I barely left the house. Waking up each day felt like living a nightmare—dark, purposeless, and consumed by hate. I hated him. I hated her. But most of all, I hated myself. Waves of emotional turmoil drowned me, and I didn't know how to surface. This relationship was a karmic relationship—a connection so powerful and painful it transforms you to your core. I loved him deeply, and being with him often felt like stepping into a magical, fairy-tale world. But the betrayal cut just as deeply. The pain left me no choice but to change.

That's when I turned to books, self-growth podcasts, and, eventually, writing as my swimming float... Slowly, day by day, I poured myself into writing to let it all out.

My writing wasn't elegant or polished—it didn't need to be. It was raw, messy, and unapologetically real. I began writing letters to my past self, with honesty, compassion, and, at times, frustration. These letters became a mirror, reflecting truths I had avoided and feelings I had buried.

Here's what I learned: When you write to yourself, you're not just letting the emotions flow—you're observing your thoughts from a distance. You begin to see patterns in your thinking, recognize the lies you've told yourself, and realize the truths you've been avoiding. It's a slow, step-by-step process, but every word you put on paper is a step toward transformation.

In the next section, I'll show you an example of how I started writing to myself. This practice is simple but very powerful, and it's one of the tools that helped me to shed the skin and rebuild my confidence.

Here is the small section of the letter I wrote to my past self at that time:

"*I understand you have fears, flaws, and moments of selfishness. You've been stubborn, doubtful, and afraid of judgment. But despite all that, I know you've been doing your best. You've faced the world, even when you felt unprepared or insecure.*"

When I reread these lines, something clicked. I realized that I had defaulted to viewing myself negatively. I was using phrases like "I understand" and "I know" because I was scared of the unknown, craving control over my emotions (the egotistical self). The process of writing this letter revealed an internal narrative I hadn't fully faced—one where I made excuses for myself to avoid digging deeper into the emotions I feared the most.

But here's the power of **this step**: it's the first step toward real, positive transformation. When you confront your truths with compassion, you open the door to growth. You can't rewrite your story unless you first acknowledge the parts of it that weigh you down.

Where Change Begins

Acknowledgment doesn't mean accepting defeat or dwelling in self-pity. It means being kind enough to yourself to see things clearly. Yes, you've made mistakes—everyone has. But self-hatred won't fix the past. Worrying about what you can't change won't help, and fear is nothing more than a mirage. All we really have is *this moment*. Right now, you have the choice to be more understanding, forgiving, and kind to yourself and others.

In the next part of my letter, I wrote:

"Let's choose loving kindness. Forgive yourself for your mistakes and start forgiving others for theirs. Everyone is doing their best, just like you. We all carry our own burdens, and more often than not, we're far harder on ourselves than others are. It's time to stop blaming yourself for things you couldn't control."

Writing this letter was a breakthrough for me. It helped me realize that while positive self-talk has its place, it's not enough. Healing doesn't come from just feeling better temporarily. It comes from taking **responsibility**. It's not about ignoring the past or sugarcoating reality. It's about **deep reflection**—understanding what happened, why it happened, and how you can move forward with clarity and purpose.

Unwiring the Pain Circuit

Through this process, I uncovered blind spots I hadn't noticed before. I realized how often I avoided true responsibility for my actions. I wasn't fully processing the lessons behind the pain; I was simply trying to move past the discomfort as quickly as possible.

True self-honesty requires more than just acknowledging the uncomfortable emotions we feel; it demands that we sit with them, fully embrace them, and learn from them. What does that mean in practical terms? It means allowing ourselves to feel every uncomfortable sensation instead of numbing, distracting, or avoiding them. It's about leaning into the very feelings we often run from—whether it's fear, shame, guilt, or vulnerability—and letting them speak to us, not silence us.

Embracing these emotions is like standing in the rain without an umbrella. At first, it's uncomfortable. The instinct is to seek shelter, to run and escape. But as you allow yourself to stand there, something shifts. You stop resisting the rain and begin to feel it in a new way. You notice its coolness, its rhythm, and eventually, you realize it's just rain—it won't destroy you. In the same way, **sitting with painful emotions** allows us to **see them for what they really are: messengers, not monsters.**

One of the most powerful outcomes of this exercise was the ability to **unlearn** the stories I had been telling myself about my past. By rewriting these stories, I detached the emotional weight that had been attached to them for so long. **With new stories came new thoughts, and with those thoughts, new emotions.**

This is the essence of transformation: realizing that you are not bound by the narratives of your past. You have the power to reshape them and create a new story—one that is rooted in truth, growth, and self-compassion.

Those who are unaware they are walking in darkness will never seek the light.

Bruce Lee

Here's the key: **emotional pain is not your enemy. It's your teacher.** When you choose to embrace it, you learn from it. And when you learn from it, you begin

Unwiring the Pain Circuit

to be liberated from it—not by erasing it, but by transforming it. You no longer let those negative memories and emotions dictate your actions.

Let's bring everything into focus. The journey of unwiring the pain circuit is a profound act of reclaiming your power—step by step, breath by breath. It begins in silence, where for just five to fifteen minutes a day, you create space for reflection, allowing yourself to release the weight of old emotions. Silence becomes your sanctuary, the place where you confront the lies that have kept you small. Then, nature becomes your healer. It's not just a walk in the park—it's a communion with something far greater than your struggles. The vastness of the earth absorbs your negativity, allows you to listen to your inner truth, and returns you to a place of grounded strength.

Why This Fortress Matters

Without this foundation, you'll find yourself running in circles, exhausting your energy, and falling deeper into the traps set by your Inner Lies. Emotional pain, when left unchecked, festers and multiplies. It clouds your judgment, drains your confidence, and keeps you trapped in a cycle of self-sabotage.

In the next chapter, I will guide you through the art of engaging directly with your Inner Lies. We'll move beyond simply resisting them—we'll learn how to manipulate and dismantle them entirely. Before we get there, remember this: the strength to confront your Inner Lies isn't something you're born with—it's something you build. And you've already taken the first step.

This is your turning point, unwiring the pain that has kept you trapped. Each moment of seeking silence, each walk in nature, each act of seeking reset, unlearning, and rewriting rewires your mind and frees your spirit. And watch as your life transforms—not because the world changes, but because you do.

3

How to Use Lies to Manipulate Lies

NOW THAT YOU'VE built your internal strength to stand your ground, it's time for the real battle to begin—this time with strategy and precision. Imagine yourself as a master tactician stepping into an arena, not with swords or shields, but with the sharpest weapon of all: your mind. Your opponent isn't an external force. It's the insidious voice within—way more dangerous and detrimental to your success.

Think of this like mental judo, a form of combat where you don't meet force with force. Instead, you redirect the energy of your opponent—your doubts, fears, and insecurities—using their momentum to your advantage. Every sneaky whisper of failure, every nagging thought of inadequacy, can become the fuel for your retaliation. You don't suppress these thoughts; you manipulate them into working for you. The secret to winning this battle lies in finesse, not brute force. It's about taking a skill you already have—manipulation—and using it not to deceive others but to take control of your own mind. The lies your inner saboteur tells you? They're already there, planted by external forces, absorbed over time, and disguised as truth. Instead of letting these lies paralyze you, you turn them upside down. You flip them on their heads and make them serve you. And the secret to mastering this skill? Repetition. Just like external forces have been brainwashing you with negativity, you can brainwash yourself—but this time, with intention and purpose. Through deliberate practice, you'll rewire those false narratives into unshakable affirmations.

We've all been manipulated for years—just in ways that tear us down instead of lifting us up. We've let external sources—our environment, media, judgments from others—plant seeds of self-doubt, whispering lies. These lies have wrapped us in invisible chains, quietly holding us back from our potential. **But here's the thing: what's been used against you can be turned into your greatest weapon.**

Your mind is a master manipulator, but it doesn't have to be your enemy. In this chapter, we'll dive deep into the specific ways your thoughts try to control and limit you.

We'll uncover the hidden tactics your Inner Lies use to manipulate your perspective, and, more importantly, I'll show you how to identify these traps and dismantle them. This is the chapter where you learn to turn the voice of sabotage into a voice of strength. It's time to stop being a prisoner to your thoughts and start being the creator of your destiny. Let's get to work.

Define the Act of Manipulation

You might not realize it but every one of us are all good at manipulating. Manipulation is a natural human instinct; we've been doing it since birth. When we were babies, we cried to get attention or food. That was manipulation in its most innocent form—we were learning to shape the world around us to meet our needs.

Whether in love, friendships, or at work, people use manipulation—consciously or unconsciously—to influence outcomes. A baby cries to get attention, a brand uses clever marketing to dominate a market, and an individual might charm others to get ahead socially. This isn't inherently good or bad; it's simply how humans operate.

In the World of Business and Marketing

Think about the world of business and marketing. Brands constantly manipulate consumer emotions to get attention and drive sales. Have you ever noticed how breaking news or dramatic headlines grab your focus immediately? It's because our minds are wired to react to intensity. News outlets understand this, and they skillfully manipulate that instinct to draw you in. The more shocking the headline, the more likely it is to dominate your attention—and in the world of manipulation, attention is power. Whoever controls attention, controls the outcome.

Humans, like animals in the wild, are constantly adapting and competing. If you observe wildlife, you'll see that nature is abundant but harsh. Animals compete for food, shelter, and survival. Similarly, we compete for success, love, and security in our own lives. We manipulate situations—whether it's in the workplace, relationships, or even social interactions—to get what we want or need. It's a survival tactic that's hardwired into our DNA and creates the society around us.

Now, manipulation may sound like a harsh word, but it's important to understand that it's neither inherently good nor bad. **It's a tool.** And just like any tool, it can be used in positive ways or negative ways. The key is learning to manipulate our own internal lies to serve us, not manipulate others to achieve personal benefits.

The Twisted Manipulation

Throughout history, manipulation has been used in destructive ways, especially when the goal is to control others for personal gain. Whether it's attention, money, fame, or status, manipulating others for selfish reasons might bring short-term success but always comes with a price. It leads to a vicious cycle of lies, addiction, and suppression. Why? Because we're focusing on controlling things *outside* of ourselves—something humans are not wired to do.

Think about how draining it is to constantly worry about what others think, to predict the future, or to dwell on the past. We waste our energy trying to control things that are out of our reach, which only leads to frustration, stress, and eventually emotional burnout. It's exhausting because it works *against* our nature. If we were wired to control everything outside of ourselves, we'd be able to read minds, prevent every misstep, and avoid all pain. But we can't. And it's this attempt to control the uncontrollable that creates the emotional pain we experience—stress, addiction, anxiety, and depression.

Here's the biggest misconception: **We think we gain power by manipulating others. But the truth is, our greatest power comes from manipulating ourselves.** When we turn manipulation inward, we begin to master our own thoughts, emotions, and actions.

Imagine the energy spent trying to steer people around you, adjusting their behavior to fit your expectations or constantly reshaping yourself to keep them happy. You feel content when they align with your wishes, but disheartened and disappointed when they don't. Or perhaps, you go along with what others want, only to find they keep pushing, stepping over boundaries, and expecting you to compromise further. It's an exhausting cycle, one that drains your spirit and leaves you feeling hollow.

This is why manipulation is closely linked to the three main causes of emotional pain: **suppressions, assumptions, and lies.** When people manipulate, they act in ways that aim to achieve a specific goal, often at the cost of truth or authenticity.

How to Master Self-Manipulation

Let's dive into a practice that has been misunderstood and misused for centuries—manipulation. The truth is, manipulation isn't inherently good or bad. Here, we'll focus on turning this tool inward, transforming it into a weapon of liberation rather than destruction. When we master this art, we become the master and the Inner Lies become the prisoner, we dominate and they submit, we command and they obey.

The first step to mastering manipulation—whether of someone, something, or your own mind—is to weaken its grip. Why is this step crucial? Because anything strong enough to dominate you cannot be easily controlled. To truly take charge, you must first strip away its power, making it pliable to your influence.

PART 1: WEAKEN THE INNER LIES

1. Identify the Inner Saboteur

The very first step in mastering self-manipulation is to **identify and observe when the Inner Saboteur is taking control.** This requires tuning into the most honest messenger you have—your body. Everything starts with the mind and your mind creates the emotions and it signals to the body. Your body is the receiver, it doesn't sugarcoat or rationalize; it reacts, loud and clear, to the thoughts coursing through your head.

Think of your body as your personal security system. When something isn't right in your mind, it sends out alarms.

- **Anxiety?** Your hands may tremble or your chest may feel heavy.
- **Self-doubt?** You may notice shallow breathing or an ache in your shoulders from the weight of overthinking.
- **Fear of judgment?** Your stomach might churn, or your jaw might clench without you realizing it.

Other symptoms such as headaches, cold hands, numbness, nervous sweating—are your body's way of signaling that the Inner Lies are tightening their grip. These are not random reactions—they are your body's way of saying, "Pay attention! Something is off."

These physical reactions are proof that your Inner Lies are manipulating and overpowering your mind and body. Think about those moments when fear grips you

How to Use Lies to Manipulate Lies

so tightly that your body reacts physically: your palms sweat, your heart races, your hands tremble, or your mind spins with anxious thoughts like: *Why did I say that? What if they think I'm stupid? Am I not good enough? What if they're lying to me? Do they hate me? They rejected me.* These are the signs of your Inner Lies in action—they are manipulating you so much that they make your body scream. When most people experience these signs, they reach for quick fixes—painkillers, distractions, or diving deeper into the spiral of anxious thoughts. They believe the narratives running wild in their minds. But here's the reality—they're falling into the trap, letting those Inner Lies dominate themselves.

2. Get Aggressive with the Inner Voice

The first step to breaking free is **awareness**. When your body sends those distress signals—when your hands sweat, your heart pounds, or your mind spirals into darkness—pause and confront it head-on. Tell your brain, **"Darn you, brain! Others might try to mess with me, but I won't let you do this to myself!"** Yes, you must be bold, this act of standing up to your own mind is the first and most crucial move in reclaiming your power.

Think about it: most people fall into the trap of fear and overthinking because they take these inner lies as gospel truth. They don't realize that even though the toxic voice lives in their own mind, it isn't their ally—it's their worst enemy. Just because it comes from within doesn't mean it's looking out for you. In fact, it can be the sneakiest, most destructive force, precisely because it disguises itself as *you*. That's why so many people feed into their Inner Lies—they don't distinguish between their *truth* and their *toxic narratives*.

But when you get aggressive with that voice, when you call it out for what it is—a liar and a bully—you'll notice something incredible. It starts to shrink. It becomes a whim, a whisper, a fleeting nuisance. Just like you'd get stern or aggressive with someone crossing your boundaries, you have to treat your inner saboteur the same way. You must declare your space and refuse to let it invade.

I know this might sound strange—**after all, it's your own brain you're arguing with—but trust me, it works so well.** When you challenge the lies head-on, when you refuse to give them the weight they crave, you'll feel the pressure lift. That pounding headache? It begins to fade. That draining sense of hopelessness? It starts to dissolve.

How to Use Lies to Manipulate Lies

Here's why: When other people try to manipulate you, they do it through their actions and words, planting seeds of doubt or self-judgment in your mind to serve their own goals and gain their benefits. You become manipulated the moment you let their behavior take root and start influencing your thoughts. The manipulation succeeds when you can't stop replaying their actions in your head—wondering, *Why did they act like that? Are they mad at me? Did they block me? Am I a loser?*

This is how their behavior becomes a weapon, not because of what they did, but because of the thoughts it triggers in you. Those thoughts—the constant questioning, self-doubt, and overthinking—are the **Inner Lies** in action. It's no longer about what they said or did; it's about the narrative you've created around their behavior.

The Inner Lies thrive on one thing—your belief in its lies. Every time you buy into their narratives, they grow stronger, feeding off your fears, doubts, and insecurities like a parasite. This process is subtle, almost imperceptible at first, which is why so many of us don't notice it. Inner Lies work quietly, weaving themselves into the fabric of our daily thoughts until they feel like reality. And the moment you push back, the moment you declare, ***"Enough!"*** you begin to strip them of their power. When you fight back, you're not just shutting down the negativity; you're reclaiming your energy, your focus, and your life. You're showing your brain who's in charge—you. Not the lies, not the fear, not the doubt. You.

It's just like dealing with a toxic person in your life—if you don't draw clear boundaries and stand firm, they'll keep taking, keep invading, keep draining. Your inner saboteur is no different.

3. Repeat the Mantra: "Everything Is Just an Illusion."

Albert Einstein once said, *"Reality is just a mere illusion."* A statement so profound, yet so easily overlooked in the chaos of everyday life. Humans cling to the seriousness of this so-called reality, getting nervous over trivial matters, worrying endlessly about things they cannot change, and exhausting themselves in the process. But let's take a moment to unpack this: *Why is reality just an illusion?*

Think about it—can you step back into the past and change what has already happened? No. Can you leap into the future and shape it before it unfolds? No. Can you hold onto a person who isn't physically present with you right now? Again, no. You can't touch anything that is not literally in front of your eyes at the present moment. The only thing you truly have is this present moment, and yet, so much of your energy is spent on things that exist only in the abstract —the past and the future.

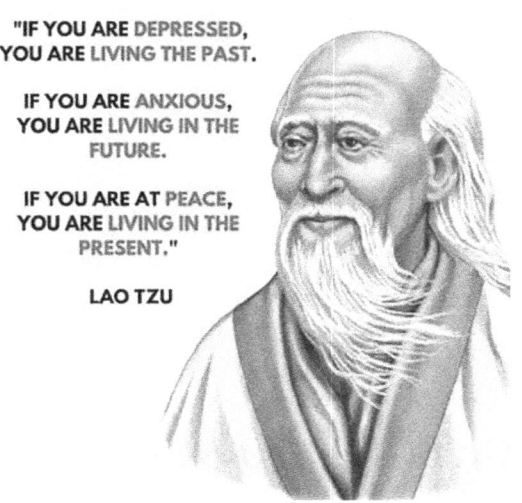

"IF YOU ARE DEPRESSED, YOU ARE LIVING THE PAST.

IF YOU ARE ANXIOUS, YOU ARE LIVING IN THE FUTURE.

IF YOU ARE AT PEACE, YOU ARE LIVING IN THE PRESENT."

LAO TZU

Your fears, your worries, your overthinking—they're all illusions. And your thoughts, many of them are your greatest enemies—These Inner Lies thrive on your inability to see clearly. They grow stronger when you treat your worries as truth and allow them to define you.

When you recognize this, you weaken the grip of the Inner Lies. You see through their façade and stop giving them the power to control you. **These insidious whispers of fear and insecurity dread one thing the most: a**

strong, confident mind that sees life with clarity. When you step into this clarity, you strip away the layers of illusion that keep you stuck and scared.

So, whenever the Inner Lies begin to creep in, when doubts cloud your vision or fears weigh heavy on your soul, pause and remind yourself: *"This is just an illusion."* That simple truth will be your compass, guiding you out of the maze of overthinking and into a life of clarity and strength. The illusion dissolves, and you take back control.

We've already pinpointed three practical steps to weaken the Inner Lies. Now, it's time to take things to the next level—to uncover the strategic art of manipulation and use it to dismantle those lies entirely. This isn't about manipulation in the traditional sense; this is about reclaiming your emotional power by mastering your inner narrative.

PART 2: MANIPULATING YOUR OWN MIND

Your own mind is a powerful thing in this universe for you. It can be your greatest ally or your most formidable enemy. By mastering the art of self-manipulation, you reclaim control. You silence the inner critic and amplify the voice that believes in you. You begin to write your own story, one where you're not just surviving but thriving.

Manipulation Strategies

Now, let's dive into how you can manipulate that Inner Lies in your own mind:

When It Tries to Demotivate You

When it says, "*You've failed before, so why bother?*" hit back with a simple fact: "**Failure is a stepping stone, not a life sentence.**"

> <u>Manipulation strategy</u>: When the demon's voice creeps in, whispering, "*You're a loser,*" or "*You're ugly,*" or ""*You've failed,*" hit back with raw defiance: **"Define failure. You are lying. I don't fail, I learn, I only fail when I stop trying."** Challenge that negativity with all the boldness you've got. You'll be surprised how quickly that inner critic starts to lose its grip when you stop entertaining its nonsense.

When It Tries to Sweet Poison You

When the demon's voice tries to sweet poison you, it doesn't come with harsh criticism or doubt. Instead, it whispers seductive lies that sound comforting, even flattering. It says things like *"You deserve a break; why work so hard?"* or *"You've earned the right to take it easy—no one else understands how much you've already done."* or *"You can do it tomorrow."* It strokes your ego, making laziness and procrastination feel justified. It tells you to indulge in distractions, to take shortcuts, to delay what matters most under the guise of self-care.

But this sweet poison is just as dangerous. It's the kind of voice that tricks you into settling for mediocrity, convincing you that it's okay to stay in your comfort zone. When it whispers, *"You're better than them,"* it's not lifting you up—it's trying to separate you from others, to isolate you in a bubble of superiority and complacency.

And what about when your ego sneaks in, smugly telling you, *"Others are idiots,"* or *"I know everything, and no one else does?"*

<u>Manipulation Strategy</u>: Don't let it fool you. Playfully but firmly, ask it, **"Do you know how much dust exists in the universe? Do you know if**

How to Use Lies to Manipulate Lies

the stock market will be up or down tomorrow? You can only guess, no one knows and you think you are smart" Let that simple question unravel the arrogance.

And when the demon tries to convince you, *"I'm the best, I know everything," or "I can do it tomorrow,"* sweetly disarm it by saying, **"How much you are making compared to Elon Musk, you guys both have twenty-four hours a day."** In an instant, you've flipped the script.

This approach isn't about tearing yourself down; it's about grounding yourself in truth. When you feel bad about yourself, *it is not you*. It's the result of the negative forces around you—external environments that drain you, and the Inner Lies you've unknowingly absorbed. Let me repeat this because it's *that* important: when you feel unworthy, anxious, or inadequate, *it is not you*. It's the echoes of toxic surroundings and the false narratives planted in your mind. The real you is never the sum of these lies. The real you is powerful, resilient, and worthy of everything you dream of.

Your New Self

When It Makes You Feel Unloved or Betrayed

Let's say you're in a situation where someone has betrayed you—they may have cheated, lied, or spoken badly about you behind your back. Naturally, you start feeling hurt, inferior, or even worthless. Thoughts flood your mind: *I am wrong. I am such a bad person. I'm not good enough. I'm ugly. What if they leave me?* These negative voices are your inner demon feeding on your pain, making itself stronger by pushing you further down.

But here's the truth—it's not the other person who makes you feel this way. It's your own mind turning against you. So how do you manipulate this situation for your benefit?

> **Manipulation Strategy:** Instead of letting these destructive thoughts take over, turn your focus inward and take back control. Say to yourself, **"Hey, brain—why are you trying to talk down on me?"**

Then tell yourself: *"So what? If I make mistakes, I fix it. What's the big deal? Life is all about overcoming mistakes."*

By doing this, you're pulling the power away from those toxic thoughts and asserting control over your mind. You'll notice how this immediately shifts your energy. You're no longer feeling weak or powerless; instead, you've reclaimed your inner strength. The key is to be more assertive than the negativity trying to dominate you.

When It Makes You Feel Stuck in Regret or Sadness

We've all had moments where something from the past haunts us—whether it's a betrayal, a mistake, or a painful loss. In these moments, your inner voice starts whispering things like, *"I am worthless,"* or *"I failed, and life is hard."* This is the evil within trying to chain you to the past, trapping you in regret and self-blame.

How can you manipulate this voice and free yourself from its grip?

Manipulation Strategy: When that voice starts, confront it by saying, ***"The past is an illusion. I can't touch it, so it has no power over me. Every day is a gift. I'm stronger than my mistakes and I deserve success and happiness."***

This mental shift allows you to manipulate your emotions in a way that helps you move forward. You stop letting the past control you and start seeing it as just one chapter in a much bigger story. By reframing those painful memories, you regain your power.

When It Makes You Feel Worried About the Future

Let's say someone has told you that you should be worried about something coming up—a deadline, a confrontation, or a difficult decision. You start feeling anxious, maybe even terrified, because you're not sure what's going to happen. Your mind starts spinning: *"What if I fail?"* or *"What if they're right?"* The fear of the unknown can be paralyzing, but it's also the perfect moment to use manipulation to your advantage.

Manipulation Strategy: Instead of letting fear take the wheel, remind yourself of a simple truth: ***"No one knows the future, and I do not either and I choose to focus on what I can control. I deserve abundance and happiness. I am uniquely gifted."***

How to Use Lies to Manipulate Lies

Here's the key: the art of manipulating your own mind is no different from any other form of manipulation. It requires repetition, persistence, and a relentless commitment to force it to go your way. When your inner saboteur starts shouting its lies, don't retreat. Don't let it roar louder. Instead, confront it like you would a disruptive person in your life. Imagine a conversation with this voice. Get aggressive, creative, and unyielding. Talk back to it with conviction. The trick lies in consistency. You don't tame a lion in one day, and you don't overpower your Inner Lies with one rebuttal. It's a daily battle—a relentless fight for your mind and body. And you need to fight because these Inner Lies are treating you very badly in your own internal world. You must know what to say, how to say it, and never let up. You must outwit, outlast, and outmaneuver that sabotaging voice until it has no choice but to submit to your authority.

Your brain is your terrain, your battlefield, and your kingdom. Protect it fiercely. Be strong every single time those Inner Lies dare to rise. Relentlessly fight for your peace, your clarity, and your power. And most importantly, tell that part of your brain—the evil, lying part—that it's no longer in control. This is your mind, and you own every inch of it.

4

SELF: Defining Self-Love, Self-Betrayal, and Selfishness

NOW THAT YOU'VE begun to master the art of Unwiring the Pain Circuit and Using Lies to Manipulate Lies, you're starting to see just how much power you truly have over your inner demon. But the journey doesn't stop there. Each time you silence that critic within, you begin to release the emotional baggage that's been weighing you down. And here's where the magic truly unfolds: **all the energy you once spent battling those inner lies can now be redirected into something powerful**—the love to yourself—the pure, beautiful, angelic side of yourself that has always been there patiently waiting beneath the noise of self-betrayal. When you shift from fighting internal demons to nurturing this divine, loving force within, you unlock a new level of personal freedom and power. Instead of draining yourself through self-doubt, you now feed your soul with the love it deserves.

Your New Self

This chapter is all about understanding how to love yourself the right way. Now that you've silenced the inner saboteur and taken back control, it's time to channel all that reclaimed energy into building a successful and abundant future. When we misinterpret self-love, we risk falling back into the same traps set by the inner saboteur: suppression, assumptions, and dishonesty. Loving yourself the wrong way can undo the hard work you've done to dismantle the lies and break free from emotional pain.

True self-love is about being centered—staying grounded in who you are and what you stand for. It's about cultivating a sense of respect for yourself that keeps you strong against the pull of unhealthy choices or toxic relationships and habits. When you're firmly connected to your authentic self, you can confidently say no to what doesn't serve you and yes to what nurtures your soul. True self-love is not endless scrolling through social media, binge-watching movies, or distracting yourself with constant shopping and games. Those are distractions—activities that fill the void temporarily. Instead, it's about pulling away from those distractions and spending time reflecting on your flaws, your vulnerabilities, and your growth. It's an act of self-love because you're choosing the short-term discomfort of self-discipline for

SELF: Defining Self-Love, Self-Betrayal, and Selfishness

the long-term reward of true fulfillment. It's not about striving for perfection, but about embracing who you are and having the courage to grow into the person you're meant to be.

This chapter will guide you in understanding what it means to truly respect and care for yourself, not just superficially, but in a way that empowers your spirit. By staying aligned with your SELF, you'll develop the wisdom to avoid falling back into the traps of manipulation and self-sabotage. You'll learn how to make decisions that honor your growth and sustain the foundation you've built. True self-love isn't just a feeling; it's a practice, a commitment to nurture and protect the powerful, purposeful life you are born to live.

Self-Love

Self-love isn't about pampering yourself with luxury or indulging in temporary distractions, that is selfishness. Self-love isn't about inflating your ego or seeking validation from others—that's actually a form of self-betrayal. **True self-love is the act of knowing your worth and standing up for your rights.** It's knowing who you are, owning your needs, and navigating life without letting external validation dictate your worth.

For example, without facing the root of my insecurities, I would have never found the courage to speak my truth, to say no when necessary, or to humble myself enough to adjust my own behavior. This journey wasn't one of instant change, but of cultivating inner stillness and committing to real self-reflection. The idea of self-love often sounds simple, but the reality is, it requires intense discipline and a willingness to confront discomfort.

Self-Love vs. Self-Betrayal

Let's break this down further. When you seek validation from others—whether through status, money, or outward appearances—you are betraying yourself by placing your value in their hands. The more you seek approval outside, the further you stray from who you really are. That's self-betrayal. **True self-love means expressing yourself freely and honestly, without forcing yourself into roles or expectations that don't align with who you are.**

Self-Love vs. Selfishness

Now let's address a concept that often gets mistaken for self-love: **selfishness**. At first glance, they can seem similar—both centered around the self, but their roots

SELF: Defining Self-Love, Self-Betrayal, and Selfishness

are worlds apart. **Selfishness is born from ego, driven by a relentless need to prioritize your desires above everything else, even if it means hurting others.** It whispers, *"I must win, no matter the cost."* This mindset leads to manipulation and dishonesty, not just with others, but with yourself. You begin to blur the lines between what's real and what you want to believe, convincing yourself that you're protecting your own interests, when in fact, you're betraying your deepest truths.

For example, selfishness might push you to avoid difficult situations, leading you to tell white lies or spin stories to dodge discomfort. You justify it, thinking, *"This is for the best."* But every time you do that, you distance yourself from your true feelings and authenticity. It's a slow betrayal of self. You become a prisoner of your own defenses, constantly hiding behind a façade, avoiding the tough conversations that could set you free. Selfishness keeps you locked in a loop of fear and control, where you're perpetually bracing against the world instead of truly living in it.

Self-love, on the other hand, is rooted in compassion. When you practice self-love, you forgive yourself and extend that same compassion to others. With selfishness, you feel like the victim of life's circumstances—always defending, hiding, or demanding. But with self-love, you realize that you are the protector of yourself and others. You let go, you understand, and you respond to life from a place of ease rather than frustration.

For example, think back to a time when someone insulted you or criticized something close to your heart. What was your immediate reaction? Most likely, your mind went straight to defensiveness, with thoughts like, *"How dare they say that about me?"* or *"They don't even know who I really am."* These reactions are driven by ego, that inner saboteur that thrives on feelings of inadequacy and the need for external validation.

But when you reframe the situation through the lens of self-love—from a place of true compassion, the internal dialogue shifts. Instead of taking the criticism as a personal attack, you begin to ask yourself, **"Could this be more about their pain than mine?"** *or* **"How can I help them?"** *or* **"How can I make this better?"** Self-love gives you the strength to step back, detach from the emotional sting, and see the situation from a place of wisdom and compassion. You move from being reactive to proactive. **This is an act of choosing kind thoughts over resenting thoughts, of self-love because it lifts the weight off your soul.** When you're not just letting go of anger, you're freeing yourself from the toxic grip of emotional baggage that silently poisons your well-being. Pain, frustration, and anger are not just mental chains; they slowly erode your internal body system. Over time, they transform into anxiety, depression, or even chronic physical ailments. That's the heavy toll of living under the constant criticism of your inner voice.

Self-love, at its core, is an act of profound compassion and forgiveness—not for others, but for yourself. You allow yourself to let go of the urge to criticize, to judge, to cling to past wrongs. You're no longer fighting the world around you or the critic within; instead, you're creating space for healing and true liberation for your own soul.

Once you start learning to shift your resenting thoughts to forgiving thoughts. You will learn that the truth is that most people don't intend to harm—they simply don't know better, or perhaps your own lens is clouded by a judgmental mind. **With a single shift in a thought, you give yourself the power to change your life.** That simple act of compassion could be the very thing that shifts your entire reality. And that's where your power lies.

Practicing Self-Love

Here are a few exercises you can try to practice self-love and shift your reactions in everyday situations:

- **In Traffic:** If someone cuts you off, instead of getting angry, remind yourself: *"Maybe they're rushing because something happened to their loved one."*
- **With Loved Ones:** When a loved one is upset or lashes out, think: *"They might be struggling with something deeper. How can I show them compassion?"*
- **Facing Betrayal:** If a partner betrays your trust, instead of reacting in anger, reflect: *"They're acting out of their own pain or insecurities. It is not totally about me."*
- **Dealing with Criticism:** When someone criticizes you, rather than feeling insulted, ask yourself: *"What can I learn from this? They might have their reason why they said it, what they said could be partially true. How can I grow from this feedback?"*
- **Feeling Ignored:** If someone you care about doesn't respond to you, instead of taking it

personally, remind yourself: *"They may be dealing with their own struggles. It's not necessarily about me."*

Each of these situations offers an opportunity to practice self-love by changing the narratives in your mind. Instead of reacting defensively, you create space for compassion and understanding—toward yourself and others.

Habits of Self-Love

In today's fast-paced, tech-driven world, self-love habits are often the first to be sacrificed. Our attention spans are shrinking, bombarded daily by an endless stream of notifications, news, and distractions on our phones. People live faster than ever, rushing through their days without realizing they've lost the space to unplug and reconnect with themselves. This constant state of hyper-connectivity goes against our natural rhythm, leaving many feelings drained, frustrated, and out of touch with what truly makes them feel alive and rejuvenated. Many of the small, seemingly harmless actions we take each day—ignoring our well-being, pushing through exhaustion, or mindlessly scrolling—are actually contributing to a life of irritation, burnout, and dissatisfaction. I'll guide you through five simple yet profoundly impactful self-love habits that are often overlooked.

These aren't grand gestures or time-consuming rituals—they're small, intentional practices that, when embraced, can shift your entire life trajectory. By bringing these habits into your daily routine, you'll not only notice how they elevate your energy and clarity but also how they help you break free from the cycles of frustration and irritation.

1. No Complaints
2. Focusing on Small Wins
3. Reflection
4. Living Today As Your Last Day
5. Committing to Consistent Kindness

No Complaints: The Silent Energy Killer

Here's something that often gets overlooked: **complaints feel good.** They give us a fleeting sense of validation, as if by voicing our dissatisfaction, we're somehow asserting control. Complaining is like indulging in a sugary treat that satisfies in the moment but leaves you with nothing but emptiness afterward. It might make

SELF: Defining Self-Love, Self-Betrayal, and Selfishness

you feel clever or sharp, but the truth is, when you spend your time complaining, you're slowly sinking into a life of perpetual winters—cold, bleak, and stagnant.

Most of us track patterns to survive; we learn how to avoid danger and seek comfort. But when we don't track our own **behavioral patterns**, we fall into a dangerous loop. Complaining becomes a habit, a reflex. You might not even notice how often you utter phrases like, *"I'm so tired," "Why is this happening?"* or *"That's so annoying."* These complaints are like carrying around a heavy backpack, weighing you down without offering any value. You're just burdening yourself without moving forward.

When you complain without action, you're essentially standing next to a pile of trash and commenting on the smell instead of taking out the garbage. You think you're solving the problem by acknowledging it, but all you're doing is letting it fester. Complaints, without reflection or action, only prolong the problem.

In relationships, this cycle is especially common. Picture this: you vent to a friend, *"Why did she act like that?"* They nod, joining in, validating your frustration. For a brief moment, you feel seen, understood, part of a tribe. But here's the truth—your friend isn't the person in question, and they don't truly know why she acted that way. **Has anything changed through complaining? No. The problem lingers.** All venting did was offer the illusion of control while leaving you stuck in the same spot. It's like letting out steam without cooling the engine; you're burning fuel, yet going nowhere.

Complaints are like weeds that take root in your mind, occupying valuable space that could be filled with resilient, solution-oriented thoughts. When you spend time complaining, you become fixated on how stuck the situation feels, rather than focusing on how to change it. **Complaining, in essence, is giving power to the problem instead of to the possibility.** The moment you stop complaining, you start building momentum to push through obstacles and reclaim control of your situation.

Solution:

The next time you catch yourself slipping into the familiar trap of complaining, pause. Recognize that this is your brain's default reaction to discomfort, but it doesn't have to be your final one. Complaining is like taking a detour that leads nowhere—stuck in the same cycle without moving forward. But now, you hold the power to steer in a new direction.

Here's a powerful strategy. When that complaint rises up, tell your brain, *"Complaints are only for losers."* This **interrupts the negative pattern and sends a clear message to your mind that you won't tolerate defeatist thinking.** From there, shift to winning thoughts like, *"What can I learn from this?"* or *"How can I grow from this challenge?"*

As Napoleon Hill so famously said, *"Every adversity, every failure, every heartache carries with it the seed of an equal or greater benefit."* Use this as your guiding mantra. When you choose to focus on what you can gain from every setback, you instantly rewire your brain to seek out solutions rather than staying trapped in problems.

This isn't just about stopping complaints—it's about transforming your perspective and unlocking a life free from unnecessary negativity. **Complaining is a habit, and like any habit, it can be rewired.** The more you practice these steps, the easier it becomes to break the complaint cycle and shift your focus to gratitude and action. Over time, this shift will change not only your mood but also your reality. You'll find yourself feeling lighter, more in control, and empowered to create solutions instead of dwelling on problems.

Focus on Small Wins: Building Momentum with Every Step

Small wins are not insignificant—they are the foundation upon which great success is built. Each one is like a single drop of water. Individually, they may seem like nothing, but over time, those drops fill an entire ocean of transformation. Think of every small victory as a seed you plant in the garden of your life. You may not see it sprout overnight, but with time and care, it will grow into something magnificent.

Take, for example, Dwayne "The Rock" Johnson. Before becoming a global superstar, he was a struggling football player and then a wrestler. In interviews, he often talks about the importance of grinding through small victories daily. He's been quoted saying, **"Success isn't always about greatness. It's about consistency. Consistent hard work gains success. Greatness will come."** Johnson's daily routine of pushing through small, consistent efforts eventually propelled him to become one of the most recognized and successful figures in entertainment.

In the end, **small wins are the heartbeat of lasting change, much like how the small, consistent beats of your heart keep you alive.** Each tiny step—no matter how insignificant it may seem—adds up to create the rhythm of resilience. Just as a single drop of water might seem small, over time, it fills the ocean, creating a force that is powerful and unstoppable.

Solution:

Celebrate every small win in your life—no matter how tiny it may seem. Start by making small, manageable changes in your daily routine, like picking up a piece of garbage outside your door, cleaning your space, or waking up just a little earlier than usual. These are not insignificant acts—they're stepping stones to greatness.

The power lies in recognizing that progress is about small, consistent steps forward. It's not about making massive leaps overnight; it's about doing a little better today than you did yesterday. This mindset shift, however simple, matters deeply. Each small win creates a ripple effect that reinforces the belief that you're capable of more.

By embracing this mindset, you're not just moving forward—you're training your mind to seek growth and improvement every day. This is how you shift from being stuck in the ordinary to creating an extraordinary life.

Reflection: Steering the Ship of Your Life

Reflection isn't a passive activity—it's an active, intentional process of recalibrating your life's direction. It's the moment you step back, take stock, and consciously assess your actions, decisions, and experiences. Imagine yourself as the captain of a ship: without periodically checking the map, adjusting the sails, or observing the stars, you risk drifting off course. Reflection is your navigational tool, allowing you to break free from the autopilot mode of daily life and ensure you're aligned with your true purpose.

But reflection is more than just an intellectual exercise—it's an act of self-love. Think of it as a detox session for your mind. Just as you give your body a spa day, rest, or nourishment to restore its vitality, your mind deserves the same care. Reflection is your mental spa—it clears out the toxic thoughts that clutter your soul and makes room for refreshed and new powerful insights.

To break free from the cycle of unwanted behaviors, reflection is key. But not all reflection is created equal. Proper reflection isn't about **overthinking** or dwelling on past grievances; it's about **evaluating your behaviors** and deciding how to act differently in the future. It's like cleaning a window covered in dust; the clearer the

SELF: Defining Self-Love, Self-Betrayal, and Selfishness

glass, the more vividly you can see the world outside and understand how you fit into it.

Believe it or not, **as we grow into adulthood, we all betray ourselves in some way.** We lie to ourselves to feel good, lie to others to avoid discomfort, and force ourselves into roles or actions that please others but leave us feeling hollow. This is self-betrayal. And when we betray ourselves, we inevitably end up betraying others, too. It's a toxic way of living, yet so many of us unconsciously follow this path. **Why? Because deep down, we yearn to live on our own terms and be accepted for who we truly are. And reflection grants us this opportunity for our life.**

Bill Gates is the cofounder of Microsoft. Despite being one of the most successful entrepreneurs of our time, Gates is known for regularly taking what he calls "Think Weeks." Twice a year, he retreats to a remote location, away from all distractions, to reflect deeply on his work, life, and the future. During these retreats, he reads, writes, and spends time thinking about big-picture ideas and long-term goals for both his business and personal life.

These Think Weeks have been a crucial part of his ability to innovate and stay ahead in the tech world. Gates himself attributes many groundbreaking decisions, such as his foresight about the rise of the internet, to the clarity and insights gained during these periods of reflection. It's a perfect demonstration that reflection is not about dwelling on past mistakes or overthinking but a disciplined practice of stepping back, gaining perspective, and adjusting your course.

Steve Jobs was a master of this. He was known to take long walks when faced with difficult decisions, using that time to reflect on his next steps. **"You can't connect the dots looking forward; you can only connect them looking backward,"** Jobs once said. His ability to pause, reflect, and adjust allowed him to steer Apple toward revolutionary innovation time and again.

Solution:

One of the most effective ways to break free from this cycle is through radical self-honesty. This practice isn't about judgment or criticism—it's about creating a safe space for truth to surface. A simple yet powerful way to begin is by writing a letter to your past self, taking a long reflective walk in the park, or even spending an evening alone in stillness. These acts allow you to step outside the chaos of your thoughts and observe them from a gentle distance.

Another solution is reading. Dive into books from the genres you genuinely love. Don't force yourself through pages that don't interest you—you'll find that true learning and inspiration come easier when you're captivated by what you're reading. The knowledge will sink in naturally, enriching you without feeling like a chore. George R.R. Martin once said, *"I have lived a thousand lives and I have loved a thousand loves. I have walked in distant worlds and seen the end of time. Because I read."* Reading, reflecting, and challenging your own perceptions forces you to think. It helps you **unlearn** behaviors that no longer serve you, clearing the way for new growth.

Live Today As Your Last Day

"If today were the last day of my life, would I want to do what I am about to do today?" —Steve Jobs

This part of the book wasn't planned. I'm adding it because of two heartbreaking losses I experienced just last week.

The first was a friend's mother—a remarkable woman in her fifties. She was the backbone of her family: a loving mother, a devoted wife, and a brilliant businesswoman.

She worked tirelessly, managing debts and the weight of her responsibilities to sustain her loved ones. One night, everything was normal—she was healthy, still planning for the future. And then, one day I received the announcement that she committed suicide.

The second loss was a young man, just twenty-three years old, the younger brother of a dear friend. He was full of life—handsome, intelligent, and, above all, fiercely loving. He never indulged in harmful behaviors; his heart was pure, and he lived to love. Yet, overnight, he was gone.

When I heard the news, I was frozen. These two events shook me to my core. They forced me to reevaluate everything—my bucket list, my relationships, my priorities. I thought about the people I've held grudges against, the things I've put off, and the moments I've taken for granted.

Life is breathtakingly precious, yet unimaginably fragile. It's sustained by a single breath—a breath that could be your last.

Wake up every day with this mindset: **"Every day is a gift, and today could be my last day on earth."** I promise you; this mindset will transform you into the happiest person alive.

Solution:

How to Live Like Today Is Your Last Day

1. **When you're mad at someone, ask yourself:** If they were gone tomorrow, would you want to stay mad at them? Let it go. Forgiveness isn't for them—it's for you.
2. **When you're overworking or stressing yourself out, ask yourself:** If I didn't wake up tomorrow, would I regret how I spent today? Prioritize your well-being and do things that light up your heart.
3. **When you're stuck in a rut or feeling unloved, ask yourself:** What truly makes me happy? What brings me joy? Start planning how to do more of that—and act on it as soon as you can.
4. **When you're tempted to take life for granted, remind yourself:** Life is unpredictable. You never know what tomorrow holds, so make the most of today.

I'm not saying you should abandon everything you're doing right now. We still have bills to pay, kids to raise, and responsibilities to uphold. Life doesn't pause for us to figure everything out—but it does offer us moments to reflect, and that's what I'm asking you to embrace.

Take a moment to pause. Ask yourself: **Am I taking life for granted?** Are you holding onto grudges, carrying resentment, or pushing through a job that's draining your mental health? If so, it's not about quitting everything—it's about rethinking the *how*.

How can you approach life in a way that nurtures your soul instead of draining it? Sit with this question. Brainstorm. Reflect. Define what happiness means to you—on your terms and live every single day with love, gratitude, and intention.

Committing to Consistent Kindness

To master the art of kindness, especially when it feels challenging, start by manipulating the inner dialogue that fuels impulsive reactions. Your mind may instantly jump to defensiveness, anger, or judgment, especially when confronted by someone's negativity. But remember, you're in control of your thoughts, and by actively redirecting them, you can turn these moments into profound opportunities to build kindness into your life.

By choosing kindness in the face of negativity, you're telling your mind and heart that you're in

SELF: Defining Self-Love, Self-Betrayal, and Selfishness

control—that no one else has the power to dictate your emotional reality. Each small act of kindness ripples out beyond that single moment, shaping your environment and, ultimately, your destiny.

Solution:

When you're standing at the edge of reacting harshly or giving in to complaint, pause and ask yourself, *"What would kindness choose in this moment?"* This simple question acts like a mental switch, helping you reclaim control of the narrative before it slips into negativity. For example, when faced with harsh criticism, rather than letting anger and judgment fill your mind, remind yourself: *"Perhaps this person is struggling deeply in their own life. Engaging with this negativity won't serve me."* Just this single thought shifts your focus, allowing you to respond with calm instead of adding fuel to the fire.

Now consider a more personal betrayal—let's say a trusted friend tries to manipulate you, or worse, betray your trust. Instead of viewing them solely through this lens of betrayal, tell yourself, *"We've shared meaningful memories, and they've shown loyalty before. Right now, they're simply not in the right place within themselves, and that's their misfortune, but not my burden to bear at this moment."* You're not dismissing the hurt but setting clear boundaries with understanding. You honor what was positive without allowing the present behavior to drag you down. This shift allows you to keep your peace intact while limiting their impact on your life.

Kindness begins as a private act of thought, one that then shapes your words and actions. And here's the beautiful effect: **when others feel genuine kindness radiating from you, they are less likely to respond with hostility or negativity.** Even better, your act of kindness might create a shift within them, offering a glimpse of a more positive path forward. In this way, kindness becomes a silent yet powerful force that not only transforms your inner world but has the potential to change others as well.

The more you practice self-love, the more you'll see how it changes the way you respond to the world—and how the world responds to you.

SELF: Defining Self-Love, Self-Betrayal, and Selfishness

A life lesson:

Victim mentality will get you killed. No one is coming. It's up to you.

5

Building An Unbreakable SELF

UP UNTIL NOW, you've done the hard work: rewiring your inner world, dismantling the lies that held you back, reshaping your mindset, and learning how to truly love yourself. You've laid the foundation for a strong and happy self internally. And the next step is about becoming smart, deliberate, and strategic with your environment. It's about curating a space and lifestyle that elevates you, aligns with your newfound happiness, and safeguards the tremendous work you've put into your transformation.

This chapter will guide you through the process of aligning your surroundings with your internal progress, bringing everything into harmony. We'll focus on cultivating *unbreakable strength* through the *"suppleness power"*. Like the force of water—soft and flexible, yet relentless. Over time, it can carve through the hardest rock, not by brute force, but by persistence, adaptability, and an unwavering flow. This is the kind of strength we're aiming for—a balance of resilience and adaptability that makes you unstoppable, no matter the obstacle.

Let me introduce you to the **Four Dimensions of Life**—the core of who you are: **Physical, Mental, Emotional, and Spiritual.** These are not separate pieces; they are intertwined, shaping every part of your existence. When one falters, the rest inevitably suffer. They work together, constantly influencing one another, and when balanced, they propel you forward with unshakable strength. Like a high-performance machine, each of these dimensions acts as a crucial gear that drives you forward. If even one gear slips or slows down, the entire machine falters.

The same is true for your life. Every time you neglect one of these dimensions—telling yourself, *"It's just one day without exercise,"* or *"It's just one sleepless night,"* or *"I'll deal with my feelings later,"* you're letting the gears slow down. And the longer you ignore it, the louder the **Inner Lies** become, whispering, *"You're not good enough,"* or *"You are a loser,"* or *"This small indulgence doesn't matter."*

The truth is **it does matter.** Every skipped moment of self-care, every excuse to delay nurturing one of these dimensions, weakens the entire system. The whispering lies grow louder, turning into shouts, dictating your choices and stealing your power. To thrive—not just survive—you must tune and maintain all four dimensions, because they work together to create your unstoppable, resilient self.

Introduction to the Four Dimensions of Life

1. **Physical**: *"I must treat my body like a temple."*
2. **Mental**: *"No one has the right to define who I am or who I should be."*
3. **Emotional**: *"I am doing my best, and everyone is already trying their best to be happy."*
4. **Spiritual**: *"Everything happens for the best reasons."*

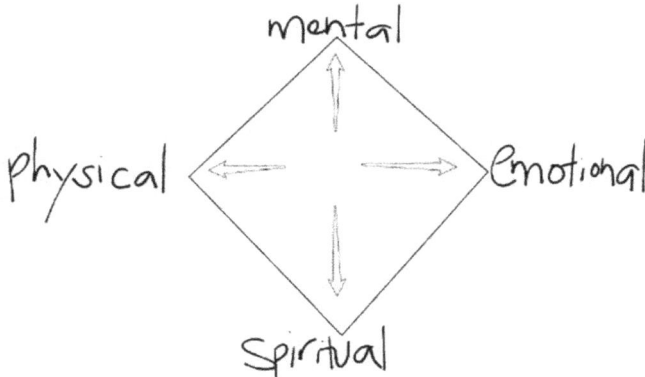

In this chapter, we'll explore how mastering each dimension leads to a state of flow where they all work together seamlessly, helping you reach your full potential.

Introduction to the Suppleness Power

Suppleness—the ability to remain **flexible yet resilient**—is one of the most powerful forms of strength. It reduces the friction in our lives, removing obstacles that we often create through our own rigid narratives and assumptions. By practicing suppleness power, we release ourselves from the mental and emotional chains that bind us, allowing us to experience peace and faith, even in times of crisis.

When the four dimensions of life are aligned and mastered, we will achieve this suppleness power because with a healthy body, you have the physical energy to move through life with ease. A stable mental state grants you clarity and focus, enabling you to make decisions from a place of determination and confidence. Positive emotions allow you to handle life's ups and downs with grace, and spiritual faith gives you a sense of purpose and understanding of the bigger picture. When all four dimensions are aligned, you become unbothered and unstoppable. When you master these four dimensions, you unlock the purest form of power—a power so subtle, it quietly threatens the very core of those still trapped in the chaos of life.

Establishing an Unbreakable SELF

The true power of suppleness is its ability to transform relationships and situations. It's not about being passive or soft, but **about mastering the balance between flexibility and toughness.**

- **Physical health** requires discipline and toughness.
- **Mental health** depends on setting healthy boundaries and standing firm in your beliefs.
- **Emotional health** comes from softness, compassion, and understanding toward yourself and others.
- **Spiritual health** is strengthened through faith and a sense of surrender.

Let's dive deeper into how to master each dimension:

1. Physical Health: "*I Must Treat My Body Like a Temple*"

As Jim Rohn said, "*Treat your body like a temple, not a woodshed. The mind and body work together. If you take good care of your body, it can take you anywhere you want to go.*"

How to Cultivate Physical Health

- **Daily Walks (Thirty minutes):**
Every single day, carve out thirty minutes for a walk. Ideally, take it in the morning, when the world is waking up and nature is alive with fresh energy. Find a trail, a park, or even a quiet street where you can feel the crisp air brushing against your skin. Let the simplicity of walking ground you—it's not just movement; it's meditation in motion. Walking in nature aligns you with something bigger than yourself. It's not just about burning calories; it's about resetting your entire system—your mind, body, and soul.

    Walking is not just a physical activity—it's a powerful ritual for emotional and mental cleansing. Each step is a small victory over the chaos inside your mind. As your feet hit the ground, imagine leaving behind the clutter of yesterday—the doubts, the worries, the noise. Feel the rhythm of your body syncing with your thoughts, aligning them toward focus and purpose. Walking allows you to open up emotionally and mentally, creating space for solutions, clarity, and even inspiration to flow in.

When you walk, your body becomes an alchemist, releasing these powerful hormones:

- √ **Endorphins:** The "happy hormone," pumps through your bloodstream, reducing pain, dissolving stress, and lifting your mood.
- √ **Serotonin:** This is your mood regulator. With each step, serotonin helps balance your emotions.
- √ **Dopamine:** heightens your sense of satisfaction and keeps you motivated.
- √ **Norepinephrine:** "focus" hormone, this is clarity booster, sharpening your focus and increasing your energy levels.

- **Healthy Diet:**
  What you eat shapes how you think, feel, and perform. Green foods and fruits are nature's powerhouse. Think of your brain like a high-performance engine—it needs clean fuel. Green foods provide that fuel by delivering consistent energy without the crash. Fish, rich in **omega-3 fatty acids (EPA and DHA)**, is vital for cognitive health. Your body can't produce these on its own, so you need them from food. Focus on **80 percent green foods and fruits**, increase your fish intake, reduce meat, and cut out white carbs. This simple shift transforms your energy, mood, and mental clarity.

- **Limit Screen Time:**
  Take a moment to think about the hours you spend staring at a screen—whether it's your phone, tablet, or computer. It's easy to dismiss, but prolonged screen time silently drains your energy and leaves you mentally and physically exhausted.

  Look around on public transport: rows of people with their heads bowed, glued to their phones, disconnected from the world around them. This overuse of technology not only limits our vitality and perspective but also takes a serious toll on our bodies.

Imagine this: as you tilt your head down to look at your phone, you're unknowingly carrying a tremendous weight on your neck and shoulders. Studies show that even a slight tilt increases the pressure on your neck by several pounds. Now, imagine carrying that weight for hours. Your brain and body are not designed to carry this invisible weight. The strain impacts your posture and causes **headaches, dizziness, fatigue, and brain fog**. At first, it feels harmless, but after hours, your body starts sending distress signals. The tension builds up, draining your energy and clouding your thoughts.

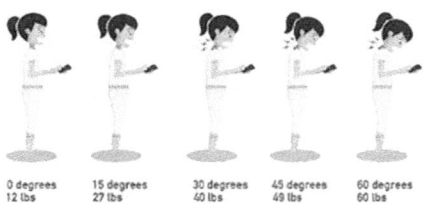

Cell phone addiction is costing us our time, our health, our relationships, and even our lives. The question we must ask ourselves is: How much more are we willing to lose?

The impact of excessive screen use isn't just about tired eyes or missed connections—it runs much deeper, affecting the very structure of your brain. **Studies have shown that prolonged exposure to screens, especially in children, can lead to a significant reduction**

in gray matter in critical areas of the brain. These are the regions responsible for regulating emotions and controlling impulses—the foundation of how we respond to life's challenges. What's even more shocking? These neurological changes mirror those seen in people with substance addictions. Yes, you read that right. Your screen habits could be reshaping your brain in ways that compromise your emotional stability and self-control. This isn't just about losing time; it's about losing a piece of your potential. So, it's time to take this seriously—not just for your focus, but for the health of your brain, your emotions, and ultimately, your life.

It's crucial for us to pause and recalibrate from time to time. **Physical health** is one of the most fundamental foundations for alleviating pain and fostering positive transformation. Without a strong and healthy body, it becomes difficult to navigate life's challenges and maintain emotional and mental well-being. Taking care of our physical health doesn't just improve our body; it creates a ripple effect that enhances our overall quality of life, providing the strength and energy we need for true personal growth.

When it comes to physical health, few embody the transformative power of discipline and resilience like

Huruki Murakami and **Tony Robbins.** Both people have shown that prioritizing physical well-being is not just about fitness—it's about unlocking the strength, energy, and mental clarity needed to excel in every area of life. Their dedication to pushing their bodies has empowered them to achieve extraordinary success and overcome incredible challenges. Let's dive into their stories to see how physical health became the foundation for their personal growth and lasting impact.

Haruki Murakami: The Intersection of Running and Writing Success

Haruki Murakami, the acclaimed Japanese author, isn't just known for his novels like *Norwegian Wood* and *Kafka on the Shore*—he's also an avid long-distance runner. Murakami's story is an unexpected yet profound example of how physical health can fuel success in a seemingly unrelated field like writing.

Murakami didn't start his life as a writer until his early thirties, when he left the bar he owned and decided to dedicate himself to fiction. But as the demands of writing mounted—long hours sitting at a desk, deep mental focus—he realized that if he didn't take care of his physical health, his creativity and productivity would suffer. He began running to clear his mind and keep his body strong, and soon enough, running became an integral part of his daily routine.

In his memoir *What I Talk About When I Talk About Running*, Murakami explains how the discipline he cultivated through running helped him maintain the stamina necessary to write lengthy, complex novels. Running taught him patience, endurance, and mental toughness—the same qualities he needed to face the blank page every day. His routine of running ten kilometers a day and participating in marathons allowed him to keep a sharp mind and balanced emotions, which translated into the clarity and focus required to create world-renowned literature.

Murakami's example shows that physical health isn't just about the body—it's deeply tied to the mind. By mastering the physical challenge of running, Murakami mastered the mental challenge of writing. **His story is a powerful metaphor: the road to success requires both physical and mental endurance.** When we nurture our physical health, we find the strength to face whatever challenges lie ahead, one step at a time.

Tony Robbins: The Role of Physical Health in Peak Performance

Tony Robbins, a world-renowned life coach and motivational speaker, is famous for his high-energy presentations and transformative personal development strategies. But few people know that his extraordinary energy comes from a disciplined commitment to physical health. He has a strict regimen of exercise, diet, and even uses cryotherapy to help maintain his vitality and stamina.

Robbins often says, ***"Emotion is created by motion."*** His philosophy is simple: **by moving the body and engaging in physical activity, we change our emotional state and enhance our mental clarity.** He believes that our physical well-being directly influences our mindset and how we show up in life. His physical health routine fuels his ability to perform at peak levels, deliver powerful speeches, and connect with audiences for hours on end.

Robbins's story proves that physical health is not just about looking good—it's about feeling good and having the energy to pursue your goals with intensity and passion. His commitment to his physical health allows him to serve millions of people around the world and maintain the focus needed to run multiple businesses.

2. **Mental Health:** *"No One Has the Right to Define Who I Am or Who I Should Be"*

We live in the information age, where information can both empower and overwhelm us. Constant consumption of information drains our mental energy and often limits our perspective. Instead, the first step to mastering mental health is redefining reality.

How to Cultivate Mental Health

We are all born with instincts and intuition, and deep down, we already have all the answers. But the distractions of life—overuse of technology, expectations, obligations, and societal norms—condition us to live from a place of logic rather than intuition. Cultivating mental health is about giving ourselves the time to listen, to feel, and to reconnect with what our mind and heart are trying to tell us.

If life is hectic, try to spend just **five to ten minutes of quiet time each day** listening to yourself. You have the answers within you, but it requires a commitment to silence and reflection. For example, when I wanted to change my habit of being indecisive, the first step was **accepting** that I was indecisive. Instead of denying it, I acknowledged that indecision wasn't serving me or my success.

Step 1: Reclaim Your Inner Power

The first mindset shift I made was telling myself, ***"No one has the right to decide what is right for me, except me."*** In the past, I would seek advice from others constantly, feeling uncertain about my own ability to make decisions. But once I began affirming this belief to myself every day, I noticed a significant change. I didn't feel the need to ask for others' opinions as much. I valued advice as a reference, but I stopped giving it the power to define my choices.

I also began telling myself that ***"no one knows anything for sure, everything is an assumption."*** This helped me develop **selective listening**, where I could hear advice without letting it control my decisions. I learned to trust my inner voice. This is key to mental health: **the ability to hear outside opinions but to make decisions from within.**

Step 2: Eliminate Outside Noise

Mental clarity cannot thrive in an environment filled with negative information and external noise. I started reducing my exposure to news about violence or scandals, realizing how it affected my mindset. **To cleanse your mind**, you need to minimize the intake of toxic information. If you feel fear or discomfort in certain situations, that's a signal your mind and heart are sending you. It's important to listen to these signals and give yourself the silent time needed to process them. Only when we create quiet spaces in our day can we fully hear the answers that are already within us.

Step 3: Reframe the Situation

One habit I struggled with was **judging others**. It was toxic, and I knew it was holding me back. To change this, I started consciously thinking **positive thoughts** about others—even if they weren't always true. For example, if someone wronged me, like stealing money, I told myself, *"Maybe they're going through something terrible, like needing money for a family emergency."* By **reframing the situation**, I found peace, which liberated me from the frustration. This wasn't about excusing others' behavior; it was about giving myself emotional freedom.

When someone betrayed my trust, I reminded myself, *"They may have already tried their best, or perhaps I did something that broke their trust too."* This mindset didn't absolve them of responsibility but allowed me to **take control of my emotions**. We all interpret situations differently, and some of us need more time to reflect and feel stable. If you find yourself feeling unsettled, give yourself more silent time each day to reframe the situations and practice loving thoughts. The hardest part of overcoming judgment is accepting our own flaws and extending that acceptance to others.

Step 4: Letting Go of the Need for Validation

I also used to crave **validation from others**. I would go out of my way to get attention, from learning how to flirt to wearing excessive makeup, just to feel seen. I'd spend money on gifts for family, hoping for recognition. But I didn't recognize these patterns until I started journaling. Writing down my thoughts allowed me to be brutally honest with myself. I realized that I gave others the power to define me because that's how I was raised—listening to others, especially my mother, 100 percent without question.

In the process of writing to myself, I asked, *"Why do I seek validation? Why do I let others determine who I am?"* It became clear that this habit was rooted in my upbringing, where I always sought approval from those

I trusted. When I finally acknowledged this, I began reclaiming my power.

As we explore the path to cultivating mental health, it's clear that defining yourself on your own terms is crucial. **Bruce Lee** is a powerful example of this. His journey reminds us that mental health begins with owning who we are, free from the expectations of others and being disciplined and selective in our surroundings. Let's take a closer look at their stories and the lessons they offer.

Bruce Lee – The Mastery of Mind through Minimalism

Bruce Lee is most often remembered as a martial arts master, but his mastery of the mind and environment is equally as impressive as his physical abilities. **What set Bruce Lee apart wasn't just his skill in martial arts, but his ability to cultivate extreme mental clarity by carefully curating his environment.** He famously practiced minimalism—not just in his physical surroundings but in the way he allowed thoughts, people, and distractions into his life.

Bruce Lee believed that mental clutter was as dangerous as physical weakness, and he worked diligently to clear his mind of anything that didn't serve his personal growth. He adopted a philosophy of "**less is more**," simplifying not just his movements in martial arts but also his approach to life. He once said, "*Absorb what is useful, discard what is not, add what is uniquely your own.*" This reflects how intentional he was about the thoughts he allowed into his mind and the people he allowed into his circle.

During his training, Bruce Lee practiced a form of mental silence—he wouldn't just fight opponents physically; he would first conquer his own mind, eliminating fear, doubt, and any external influences that could disrupt his focus. By creating this kind of mental sanctuary, he turned himself into one of the most disciplined and focused athletes the world has ever known.

What makes Lee's example so powerful is that his philosophy goes beyond martial arts. It applies to everyday life. By removing unnecessary distractions—whether they are people, habits, or even thoughts—Lee was able to channel all his energy into his craft and ultimately achieve greatness. **His story teaches us that mental strength isn't just about what we add to our lives—it's often about what we consciously choose to leave out.**

This story reflects a truth that many overlook: your environment matters. Who you surround yourself with and what you allow into your mind shapes your reality. If you want to protect the power you've built internally, you must be just as intentional about your external world. **The distractions, the toxic relationships, the endless consumption of negative information—they are all cracks in the foundation of your power.** It's easy to overlook how these seemingly small things add up over time, but the truth is, they weaken the very core of the strength you're building.

Just as water takes the shape of the container it's placed in, your mind takes the shape of the environment you allow it to operate in. By **selectively listening** and **curating the influences around you,** you can **shape your own narrative, dominate your mind, and create a life of unbreakable strength.**

3. Emotional Health: *"I Am Doing My Best, and Everyone is Trying Their Best, Too."*

Emotional health plays a critical role in our overall well-being, and it begins with two key steps: **detoxing** from negative emotions and embracing **acceptance**. This process allows us to free ourselves from internal struggles and cultivate emotional resilience, helping us to live in harmony with ourselves and others.

How to Cultivate Emotional Health

1. Emotional Detox

Before we can reach acceptance, we must first release the negative emotions that weigh us down. Emotional detox is essential to clearing out the toxic energy we accumulate through stress, frustration, anger, or pain. These emotions, if left unchecked, become trapped inside us and can lead to unhealthy reactions. Activities like shouting, crying, talking it out, running, boxing, or even chopping wood can serve as powerful tools for emotional detox.

We are often conditioned to suppress our emotions as adults, but we must unlearn this habit. Naturally, **when we are sad, we cry; when we are angry, we yell.** These reactions are normal and necessary for emotional release. What's important is finding healthy ways to express these emotions without negatively affecting others. This release is not about losing control; it's about **regulating** how we let go of bad energy to create space for positive energy.

2. Acceptance

Once we have detoxed from negative emotions, we create room for **acceptance**. Acceptance is about forgiving ourselves and others for past hurts, frustrations, and mistakes. It is the cornerstone of emotional health, allowing us to live without constantly swinging between denial and impulse.

Acceptance means being honest with ourselves and acknowledging our flaws without judgment. It also means understanding that others are doing the best they can, even when their actions hurt or disappoint us. As we embrace this mindset, we stop reacting impulsively, seeking revenge, or demanding control. Instead, our actions are driven by empathy and understanding.

Acceptance is achieved by **reframing** how we think about others and ourselves. One of the most powerful tools in this process is reminding ourselves that **everyone has good intentions**, even when their actions seem hurtful. People may lie, betray, or manipulate, but these behaviors often stem from their own pain or blind spots.

When negative emotions like jealousy or anger arise, **pause**. Instead of reacting impulsively, count slowly from one to ten, and as you do, tell yourself positive or compassionate thoughts about the person or situation.

For example, if someone betrayed you, tell yourself, *"They might have a personal reason that it is really hard for them to share,"* **or** *"There might be something I have not fully understood about this situation,"* **or** *"They have done me wrong but it is not necessary for me to do the same to them."* This practice helps shift your perspective and weakens the power of your ego.

In my experience, most of the negative assumptions we make about others are not true. Many times, when I thought people acted with bad intentions, it was really my own mindset projecting those fears. **We see the world through the lens of our own perceptions**, and often, those perceptions are clouded by our own biases and insecurities. By taking a moment to pause and reflect, we can separate our ego from the situation and respond with greater clarity and compassion.

3. Confidence

One of the most profound truths in life is this: **No one, absolutely no one, has the right to define who you are, how you should feel, or what your future holds.** Confidence is born from this realization, and it grows stronger every time you assert your own truth over the noise of external opinions. In a world filled with people eager to tell you who you should be—family, society, media—this is where your power lies. True confidence is not arrogance; it's an unshakable belief that you alone hold the keys to your destiny.

From the moment we are born, we are bombarded by external definitions of who we should be. These come from family expectations, societal norms, peer pressure, and even the media we consume. The first step in building unshakable confidence is recognizing when you are allowing those external narratives to shape your internal dialogue.

For example, let's say you grew up in a family that valued stability above all else. Perhaps they told you that pursuing creative work or taking risks wasn't practical. Over time, you internalize these messages, and they form the basis of your beliefs about what's possible for you. But here's the catch: **just because someone else says it doesn't mean it's true for you.**

Imagine you're an aspiring artist, but those ingrained beliefs keep whispering, *"This isn't practical. You'll never make good money from this."* To build confidence, you need to **first recognize that those words aren't yours— they belong to others.** Only then can you begin to dismantle them and replace them with your own truth.

Start each day by reminding yourself that *you* define your life. Speak it aloud if necessary: ***"No one else has the right to write my story. My path is mine alone, and I have the power to choose it."*** This is not about pretending everything will be easy—it's about standing firm in your truth, living boldly and authentically. Living boldly and authentically means being unapologetically you. It's about wearing what you want, speaking your truth, and pursuing your passions—even when others don't understand. This doesn't mean ignoring advice or being reckless; it means aligning your actions with your values, regardless of external validation. When you aggressively pursue what is right for you, you will find the ways to make it work. *"When there is a will, there is a way."*

As we explore the impact of self-talk on mental and emotional health, the journeys of **Will Smith** and **Misty Copeland** stand out. Both used positive inner dialogue to shape their experiences. Their stories demonstrate how self-talk can build resilience, transform relationships, and lead to personal freedom. Let's examine how they harnessed this powerful tool for change.

Will Smith: *"I Can Create Whatever I Want"*

Actor and entrepreneur **Will Smith** is a strong advocate for the power of self-talk and positive thinking. Smith has often spoken about how he uses mental conditioning to create the life he envisions. He believes in the idea that we have the ability to manifest our future through our words and thoughts.

Smith has said, ***"The first step is you have to believe that it's possible. The second step is you have to say it to yourself over and over. And then you have to believe that you can create whatever you want."*** His approach to self-talk is rooted in the belief that we can control our reality through what we repeatedly tell ourselves.

From overcoming the challenges of Hollywood to becoming one of the most bankable stars in the world, Will Smith attributes much of his success to his positive mindset and the way he speaks to himself. His story reinforces the idea that **self-talk is not just about positivity—it's about reinforcing your belief in your ability to shape your life.**

Misty Copeland: "My Body Tells My Story, And It's Powerful"

When Misty Copeland took center stage as the first African American female principal dancer at the American Ballet Theatre, she did more than just break barriers—she rewrote the definition of grace, power, and excellence. Growing up, she was told time and again that she didn't have the "right" body for ballet—too muscular, too curvy, too different. But instead of shrinking under the weight of those judgments, Copeland rewired her self-talk to not just accept her uniqueness, but to elevate it. *"My body tells my story, and it's powerful,"* she declared.

Copeland's journey is a lesson in defiance—not against the art form she loved, but against the voices that tried to limit her potential. **Every time she faced rejection or critique, her self-talk reinforced her belief that her differences were her strength.** *"I am not here to fit into your mold,"* she would tell herself, *"I am here to expand it."* With each performance, she didn't just dance—she transformed the stage into a platform for diversity, individuality, and strength.

Misty's internal dialogue became her armor, protecting her from a world that tried to box her in. She made the conscious choice to embrace her body, her story, and her journey—refusing to conform to anyone else's standards. **Her success teaches us that true power lies in owning every facet of who you are and turning perceived flaws into unmatched strengths.**

When you align your self-talk with your highest vision for yourself, nothing—not even the most rigid standards—can hold you back.

4. **Spiritual Health:** *"Everything Happens for the Best Reasons"*

One of my favorite quotes from the book *The Simplest Gift*: ***"Either you live life, or life lives you."*** This captures the essence of faith. If we allow fear and skepticism to rule, they become our reality—an endless cycle of self-imposed limitation. But when we hold onto faith, we recognize that each experience is a stepping stone toward something greater. We regain the power to shape our journey, turning challenges into pathways that lead to a life lived fully, rather than one dictated by past hurts or negativity.

Spiritual health is nurtured through **faith**—faith in yourself, in your journey, and in something greater than you. It's about trusting that even when things don't go as planned, even if you are suffering financially, even if you are going through a divorce or a break up, everything happens for a reason. True power lies in staying **neutral amid adversity**, it's about seeing **life as a series of events that help you become a better version of yourself rather than an eternal defeat**

Today, the media feeds this cycle by presenting inflated, unattainable images of luxury, making people believe they need more to be "enough." Social media amplifies this by triggering emotional reactions and manipulating people's fears—creating a false sense of control through curated stories. People think they're staying informed, that they know the world, but the truth is, they're being sold narratives designed to hook their attention and emotions. **Repeated exposure wires the brain to believe in these false realities, locking them in a box of frustration in life.** This cycle leaves us emotionally drained and isolated, replacing trust with a restless dissatisfaction for what we have and a yearning for what others possess.

This is where the disconnection from faith begins— they lose trust in their own path, in the unseen forces that guide them, and become prisoners to the cycle of stress and urgency.

Real faith is not about controlling every outcome—it's about releasing the need to control at all. When we let go of that need, we make room for peace and allow life's magic to unfold. In its truest form, faith is far more than belief in something greater—it's about surrendering to the grand design of your life, trusting beyond the daily grind, beyond the pressure to survive and perform. **The bigger picture encourages us to see life as a journey to be trusted, not a series of events to be controlled.** Challenges and disappointments become stepping stones for growth. Instead of worrying about outcomes or trying to control every situation, we learn to let go and trust that life has a larger plan unfolding.

Many of you might wonder, *how can I hold onto faith when the world around me constantly reinforces caution?* With betrayal and self-interest often appearing as the norm, it's tempting to sink into defensiveness. The answer to overcome this issue is: Let faith start from you first. You should think of life as a field where what you plant grows. If you approach life with trust and openness, you'll gradually attract trustworthiness and positivity in return. For example: you walk into a coffee shop, feeling irritated, and snap at the barista. What will you get back? Likely, a negative attitude from that barista. Faith works the same way. When we're skeptical toward life and people, our reality mirrors that back to us, reflecting the energy we project.

How to Cultivate Spiritual Health

Cultivating spiritual health isn't easy—it's one of the toughest challenges. However, there is a **simple secret** that makes the process effortless. The following steps will help you develop spiritual well-being by trusting the bigger picture.

1. Write Manifestation: Twelve Lines per Day

This practice has given me an **unshakable faith** in life. Every day, I write: *"I am grateful for the great sources of love, good health, wealth, abundance, and happiness flowing into my life easily and frequently."* Instead of watching social media or news, every single day, without fail, I write this same line twelve times in my notebook. While I write it, I let my mind wander in the most beautiful scenes of life that make me feel happy. I immerse myself in a feeling of genuine happiness and hope.

I've been doing this for nearly two years, and while it may seem like a small act, it's been one of the most life-changing methods for my life. This simple, repetitive practice is deceptively powerful.

Why does this work? Because **repetition rewires the brain**. By writing your intentions or gratitude daily, you reinforce the message in your brain, helping to create new **neural pathways** that embed the belief into your **subconscious mind**. Once your subconscious believes it, you believe it too, and that belief shapes your reality. According to an interview with Billy Carson on The School of Greatness, "Scientists have proved in a laboratory setting that DNA in the human body begins to rewrite itself when we write positive affirmations at least nine times and speak them out loud six times per day." And when you pour intense emotion into the visions we hold in our minds. When we do this, the energy we emit grows stronger, radiating outward and aligning us more deeply with the reality we desire, drawing it closer with undeniable force.

2. Tranquility

Start by reducing time spent on activities that drain your energy: movies, social media feeds, or absorbing negative news. Instead, wake up a little earlier to embrace the quiet of the morning or, in the evening, spend time in stillness—whether through reading, journaling, or simply sitting in silence. These seemingly small shifts open up space for tranquility to flow in, for the experience of a bigger life. In that quiet space, we give ourselves room to sense life's deeper truths, we cultivate a stronger sense of faith and inner strength.

3. **Positivity**

Instead of seeing difficulties as setbacks, reframe them as **opportunities for growth**. When something challenging happens, ask yourself, *"What is this teaching me?"* Trust that each experience is a lesson designed to help you grow. Embrace the mantra: *"Life happens for you, not to you."* As **Tony Robbins** says, the belief that life is working for you, not against you, helps you navigate through adversity with faith.

As we explore the importance of **spiritual health** and **trusting the bigger picture**, the lives of **Steve Jobs** and **Richard Branson** offer powerful examples of how faith, resilience, and inner strength can lead to profound personal and professional success. These individuals faced immense challenges, yet they remained grounded in their beliefs and trusted that every obstacle was part of a larger journey.

Steve Jobs: The Quiet Power of Faith and Mindfulness

Steve Jobs is celebrated for revolutionizing technology and design, but what many people don't realize is that his journey to success was deeply grounded in mindfulness and faith—faith not only in his vision but in the process of life itself. **His story illustrates that true power comes not just from innovation but from cultivating inner clarity and spiritual discipline.** This unique approach made him more than just a tech giant; it turned him into a master of inner peace and external success.

In his early twenties, Jobs sought answers beyond the material world, traveling to India in search of spiritual enlightenment. What he found there became a cornerstone of his life's philosophy: mindfulness, simplicity, and faith. Jobs embraced Zen Buddhism and made meditation a daily practice, which gave him the mental clarity needed to cut through distractions. *"If you just sit and observe, you will see how restless your mind is,"* Jobs once said. *"But over time, it does calm, and when it does, there's room to hear more subtle things—that's when your intuition starts to blossom."*

For Jobs, the act of sitting in silence wasn't about passivity; it was about tuning into something greater.

By calming his mind and silencing the world's noise, he created space for his intuition to lead the way. **This faith in his intuition became the engine behind Apple's game-changing products.** When the world doubted him—whether it was after his ousting from Apple or the failure of early products like the Lisa computer—Jobs never lost faith in his path. He believed that every setback was part of the journey, each misstep merely a detour to greater innovation.

What makes Jobs's story even more compelling is how he applied his mindfulness to every aspect of his work. **The simplicity of Apple's iconic designs—the clean lines, minimalism, and intuitive function—came directly from his Zen practice.** His spiritual clarity allowed him to see through complexity and focus only on what truly mattered, both in his products and in life. Jobs understood that **faith is not a passive waiting game; it's an active trust in the process, a belief that the dots will connect in the end, even if the path is unclear at first.**

Through mindfulness and a steadfast belief in his vision, Steve Jobs built more than just a company—he built a life of purpose. His story is a testament to the power of aligning inner tranquility with outer action, proving that true strength comes from within, and when harnessed, it has the ability to change everything.

Richard Branson: The Adventurous Spirit and Faith in Positivity

Richard Branson, the founder of the Virgin Group, is renowned for his adventurous spirit and relentless positivity. Branson's philosophy centers around trusting life's journey, taking risks, and embracing failures as stepping stones to success. One of his key beliefs is that faith in the bigger picture allows you to overcome fear and uncertainty.

Branson often shares how his faith in his ability to bounce back from failure has been instrumental in his success. For instance, his early business ventures, like Virgin Cola, were massive failures, but instead of allowing these setbacks to discourage him, Branson viewed them as **lessons**. He believed that every challenge was part of the broader journey, leading him closer to success.

One of his most famous quotes is, ***"You don't learn to walk by following rules. You learn by doing, and by falling over."*** His spiritual health is built on his ability to remain resilient, optimistic, and maintain faith that the bigger picture is always working in his favor, even when the outcome is uncertain.

His approach is deeply spiritual in that it centers on trust—**trusting that failure is temporary, that risk leads to growth, and that by keeping a positive mindset, we can open ourselves to new possibilities.** His success with Virgin Airlines, Virgin Galactic, and other ventures demonstrates how faith in one's ability to overcome challenges leads to long-term fulfillment and success.

Their stories are powerful reminders that when we cultivate spiritual health, we gain the strength to overcome adversity, embrace uncertainty, and move toward our greater purpose. Balancing the four dimensions of life—**mental, emotional, physical, and spiritual**—is critical not just to our well-being but our success and happiness in life. Just as a chair needs all four legs to stand, so do we need these dimensions to achieve balance and fulfillment in our lives.

I won't sugarcoat it; the journey isn't always smooth. But here's the key to keep going: faith begins with a simple thought. Something as small as, *"I am grateful for a happy family,"* or *"I am grateful for the roof over my head,"* or *"I appreciate these challenges, they are my life teachers."* These may seem like small acknowledgments, but they are the seeds of something far greater. Every day that we consciously practice these thoughts, they slowly take root, transforming into a belief. And when a belief becomes part of who we are, it naturally evolves into our lifestyle.

The moment you begin a balance in the Four Dimensions of Life, you see the world differently. Instead of seeing the glass half empty, you see it half full. **Complaining turns into gratitude, and challenges become blessings in disguise. You become a warrior, brave enough to accept and overcome whatever life throws your way.**

6

Living In the New Me

"The two most important days in your life are the day you are born and the day you find out why."
—Mark Twain

The True Change of Behavior and Identity

NOW THAT YOU'VE learned to take control of your thoughts, break free from old patterns, and build new, unbreakable strength, in this chapter, we'll delve into the way to cement and maintain the powerful version of the New You.

The Life of New You is one led by clarity, purpose, and unwavering focus. It's about becoming the leader of your own destiny and sharing that strength with others once you've conquered your inner challenges. This journey isn't just about self-mastery; it's about rediscovering the essence of who you are and understanding the "why" behind everything. Your own definition of success. Why you've felt drawn to certain paths. And most importantly, why you're here in this world. You'll find the answers that have been buried under years of conditioning—the dreams you forgot, the passions you set aside, and the unique calling that is yours alone.

Living with clarity and decisive focus is like navigating with a clear lens versus stumbling with fogged glasses. With clarity, you know where you're headed, what you need, and how to get there. Your energy is directed, your goals are precise, and your journey is efficient, purposeful, and fulfilling.

As Steve Jobs famously said, ***"You can only connect the dots looking backward."*** In other words, true alignment and purpose don't just appear—they're built, one decision at a time. When you have a clear vision and set goals to guide you, each choice you make and each challenge you overcome adds up. It's only when you look back that you realize every step served a purpose, bringing you closer to where you're meant to be.

Here are the final guiding principles I've designed specifically for you—to anchor the life of the powerful New You, a life that embodies true mastery. Imagine these principles as the roots of a deeply grounded tree, each one helping you weather life's storms while you grow taller, stronger, and more purposeful. They're the keys to a life that goes beyond merely getting by—the journey that is about carving out a life that doesn't just exist but thrives in clarity and purpose, one that carries a power that's uniquely yours.

1. Notion of 4 Ms
2. Productivity Quadrant
3. Four Pillars of Mastery

NOTION OF 4 Ms

The concept of the 4 Ms was a game-changer for me the moment I first encountered it in an interview on the *School of Greatness* podcast. It felt like a wake-up call, a fresh lens through which success, not as a one-size-fits-all, but as a deeply personal journey. The 4 Ms give us the tools to define our own definition of success, to design a life that aligns with our own values and aspirations.

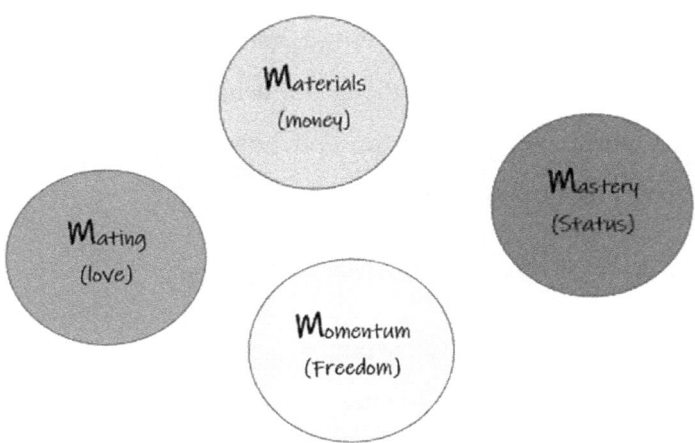

The notion of the 4 Ms redefined success. It's a concept that urges us to take ownership of our personal definition of fulfillment. Many believe that success equals money, fame, or status, but the truth is, success varies for everyone, shaped by unique life experiences and values. Depending on our past, our environment, and even our genetic tendencies, we prioritize these 4 M motivators differently. Some may crave freedom over relationships due to a painful history in connections, while others, having experienced poverty, may value material security above all else.

This was vividly illustrated to me by a story told by a famous psychologist: Two men, both deemed "successful" by society's standards, led drastically different lives. One was financially wealthy but had a fractured family and distant children—his drive had been business and finance, his top priorities. Meanwhile, the other man lived an average financial life but had a deeply connected, joyful family. His focus had always been on building a happy nest rather than amassing wealth. Both men were successful, yet in profoundly different ways. One achieved financial abundance, while the other cultivated relational wealth. It's like comparing apples to oranges—you can't say one was less successful than the other; they simply chose different paths based on what mattered most to them.

The 4 Ms—Materials, Mating, Momentum, and Mastery—serve as a powerful tool for identifying your personal drivers. It helps you get clear on what success means to you at this stage of your life. By defining your 4 M priorities, you create a roadmap toward your most essential goals, helping you align your time and energy with what genuinely fulfills you.

Once you're clear on which of the 4 Ms matters most to you, you can use the *Productivity Quadrant*—a tool we'll dive into in the next section—to lay out the critical actions and habits needed to move toward your chosen vision of success. This combination of knowing your core motivators and organizing your efforts empowers you to focus deeply on what truly counts, allowing you to craft a life of intentional success, uniquely your own.

PRODUCTIVITY QUADRANT

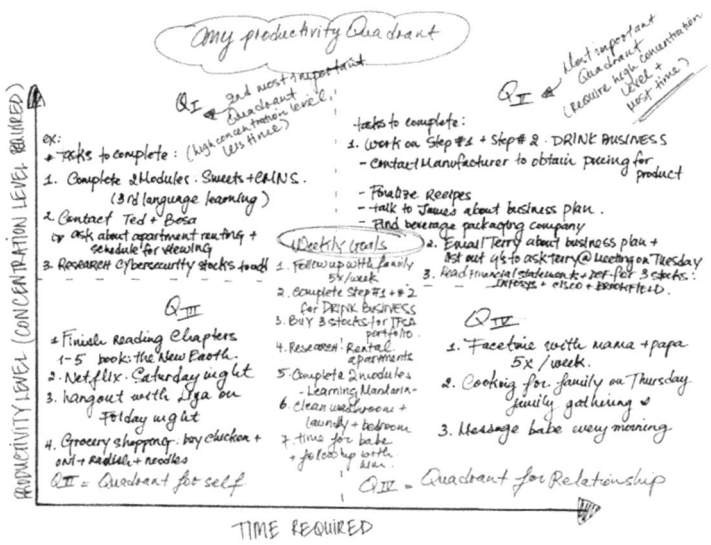

This is an example of my Productivity Quadrant.

The Productivity Quadrant: How to Actually Get Started

Let's dive into how the Productivity Quadrant can become a powerful tool for transformation and how you can take control of your time, energy, and goals. Productivity isn't just about getting things done—it's about *getting the right things done* that align with your greater vision.

This quadrant is a simple but transformative model that allows you to assess where your energy is going. It's not just about the "tasks," but the focus, intention, and consistency behind those tasks that make all the difference.

How the Quadrants Work: Simplifying and Organizing for Maximum Impact

Here's how to think about these four quadrants in a way that keeps you laser-focused on what truly matters:

Define Your Goals (Center of the Chart):

Start by clarifying your weekly, daily, or monthly goals and placing them at the center of your chart. This isn't just about jotting down tasks; it's about zooming out and seeing the broader picture of what you truly want to achieve. This is what Steve Jobs meant by: *"You can only connect the dots looking backward."* Having your key goals defined lets you connect the dots backward, aligning each small step with your bigger vision. Whether your goal is career growth, personal well-being, or creative pursuits, grounding yourself in these priorities brings clarity.

1. **Quadrant I – Fast but Crucial Zone**

   This is where you place tasks that are essential for achieving your goals but don't demand hours of your time. For example, if you're focusing on career advancement, this might include quick actions like sending an important email, following up with a colleague, or completing a short piece of research. These tasks are vital but can be handled quickly, making them the second most important quadrant. They create momentum, giving you a sense of accomplishment that drives you forward.

2. **Quadrant II – Powerhouse**

   This quadrant is the most important one, where you'll place the tasks that require deeper focus and extended time. Here lies the work that demands your attention, effort, and strategic thinking. For instance, if you're launching a business, this could include researching the industry, creating a business plan, or reaching out to potential suppliers. These tasks are critical to your success and need a substantial chunk of your time and energy. By dedicating yourself to Quadrant II activities, you're investing in the long-term goals that define who you're becoming.

3. **Quadrant III – Quick, Low Priority Activities**
   For me personally, I use this quadrant for self-care and enjoyable activities that don't require much time. These might be things like reading a couple chapters of a book, watching a short Netflix episode, or doing a quick grocery run. While they aren't central to my main goals, they help me recharge and conduct other tasks more effectively. Allocating these activities to this quadrant prevents them from taking over my day. I get the relaxation you need without letting it sidetrack my productivity.

4. **Quadrant IV – Low Priority and Time-Intensive Tasks**
   For me, this quadrant holds tasks that are meaningful but secondary to my primary focus. My current priority is my career, Quadrant IV is for nurturing relationships that don't directly advance my professional goals but are still a valuable aspect of my life. For example, cooking a family dinner, calling my parents, or planning a family gathering may fall here. These are wonderful and

fulfilling, but in seasons where career growth or personal projects take precedence, these tasks are managed after I have handled my top-priority work.

Understanding the Power of the Quadrant: Your Daily GPS

This quadrant is not just a list of tasks; it's a **compass** for where to direct your energy. Here's how to make the most of it:

1. **Review your tasks daily**: Make sure that each task contributes to the person you are becoming. Are you growing or just going through the motions?
2. **Avoid procrastination**: Procrastination is the enemy of progress. Each time you delay a task, you are reinforcing the narrative that it's okay to settle for less. You must **break the habit** of putting off important tasks by placing them in **Quadrant I and Quadrant II** and giving them your full focus.

Action Plan: Start with just **two minutes**. Get into the habit of tackling your most important task first thing in the morning, even if it's for a brief moment. James Clear's concept of the "Two-Minute Rule" (from *Atomic Habits*) suggests that **just beginning is enough to break the inertia.**

The Ripple Effect of Consistent Action

One of the hidden gems of the **Productivity Quadrant** is that it trains your brain to focus on the **right habits**, which leads to a **cascading effect** of success. Every task completed in Quadrant I and Quadrant II strengthens your ability to tackle more challenging goals. Every moment spent with intention in Quadrant III and Quadrant IV builds resilience and supports a fulfilling life.

Your life is a sum of the tasks you choose to complete or ignore each day. This **Productivity Quadrant** allows you to **align your actions with your aspirations**. Use it as your **daily GPS** to direct your focus towards what truly matters—personal mastery, growth, and meaningful success.

Remember, mastery doesn't happen in a single leap. It happens by **winning the day**—one action at a time. As Tony Robbins often says, *"It's not what we do once in a while that shapes our lives, but what we do consistently."*

By committing to your Productivity Quadrant, you're not just managing time—you're **designing your future**.

FOUR PILLARS OF A LIFE OF MASTERY

Here we delve into the Four Pillars of a Life of Mastery—principles that serve as the final blueprint to solidify the transformation you've begun. This book has been a journey of inner revelation, peeling back layers of self-doubt and dismantling the lies we tell ourselves, those deeply rooted voices that hold us back. You've learned to manipulate your own inner narrative, turning self-imposed limitations into empowering beliefs. Now, it's time to embrace a life that transcends limitations—a life where you experience the rare and electrifying joy, the profound sense of purpose and shared joy that you were born to experience. The life that you deserve to have.

The Four Pillars of Mastery Are:

1. An Organized Mind: The Blueprint for Success
2. Decisiveness: The Power of Taking Action
3. Follow-through: Bridging the Gap Between Dreams and Reality

4. The Mindset of Giving Back: Unlocking Abundance Through Service

Each pillar builds upon the work you've done so far: **an organized mind strengthens your mental clarity; decisiveness anchors your ability to act on what you've learned; follow-through keeps you aligned with your highest self even when the journey gets tough; and a mindset of giving back fills your life with meaning that goes beyond personal success.** These pillars allow you not only to sustain your newfound identity but to expand upon it, creating a life that's both powerful and purposeful.

Here, success is not just an achievement; it's the natural outcome of a mind and soul in harmony, the final liberation from the lies that once held you captive. Let's dive into these pillars and complete the journey you've started, for this is where transformation takes root and becomes the essence of who you are.

1. **An Organized Mind: The Blueprint for Success**

An organized mind goes far beyond a tidy workspace or an efficient to-do list. It's about achieving mental clarity—a state where your thoughts flow effortlessly, your goals are sharply defined, and your energy is laser-focused. Imagine your mind as the command center of your life. When it's clogged with doubts, distractions, and an endless parade of unfinished tasks, it's like trying to navigate through dense fog—disoriented and frustrated. But when your mind is organized, the fog lifts. Suddenly, the path is clear. You make smarter decisions, focus your energy on what truly matters, and begin to move through life with precision and purpose.

This clarity doesn't come by chance—it comes by design. That's where the **4 M Framework** and the **Productivity Quadrant I** introduced earlier become your greatest tools. These are not just abstract concepts; they are practical, actionable systems. Use them as your means to rise above chaos.

Here's how:

1. **Commit to practicing these two frameworks daily and weekly for at least one to two months.**
   - Every day, spend a few minutes aligning your tasks with the Productivity Quadrant.
   - Every week, reflect on how your time aligns with the 4 M priorities: Materials, Mating, Momentum, and Mastery.

Living In the New Me

2. **Watch your mind evolve.**
   At first, it may feel tedious—like learning a new skill. But soon, clarity will emerge. You'll begin to see your true desires with startling vividness. Actionable plans will naturally flow from your thoughts.
3. **Let the subconscious take over.**
   Over time, this process will embed itself in your subconscious. Your mind will start to automatically organize itself, cutting through distractions like a finely tuned machine. Planning your day, prioritizing tasks, and focusing on your goals will take less time and effort.
4. **Let it become second nature.**
   Eventually, an organized mind will become as effortless as brushing your teeth or cooking breakfast. It will no longer be something you *try* to do—it will be who you are.

True organization goes beyond physical order; it's about inner alignment. Consider someone like Elon Musk. Tackling ventures like space exploration, renewable energy, and artificial intelligence isn't just about ambition—it's his ability to structure his mind that makes it possible. Musk breaks massive visions into manageable steps, aligning his mind with each phase. This level of mental organization turns impossibilities into realities, one focused action at a time.

2. Decisiveness: The Power of Taking Action

"Indecision is the thief of opportunity."
—Jim Rohn

Decisiveness is the bridge between dreams and action. Without it, even the grandest visions remain just that—visions. To be decisive is to step boldly into action, often despite fear or uncertainty. Many people hesitate, fearing failure or judgment, but mastery demands the courage to make choices, even imperfect ones. A decision creates momentum, and that momentum builds success.

Jeff Bezos's "regret minimization" framework is a powerful example. When deciding to leave a stable job to start Amazon, he asked himself, *"In eighty years, will I regret not trying this?"* That question alone moved him past fear and into action. Decisiveness isn't about making the "perfect" decision; it's about choosing to act and learn along the way. Every decision, big or small, builds your ability to act with clarity and confidence.

3. Follow-through: Bridging the Gap Between Dreams and Reality

"99% of success is built on failure."
—Charles F. Kettering

Making a decision is the spark, but seeing it through? That's the fire. Follow-through is where the magic happens. It's easy to make grand plans or set ambitious goals when motivation is high. But what separates the dreamers from the doers, the successful from the stuck, is the relentless commitment to keep going—even when the excitement wears off, even when obstacles make you question everything.

It doesn't matter if you feel exhausted, embarrassed, demotivated, or overwhelmed by the challenges ahead. Here's the trick: **just keep showing up.** What matters is that you *do something*, however small.

- Sent that one email? You're winning.
- Wrote a single sentence in your plan? You're succeeding.
- Took one less drag of a cigarette or skipped one extra drink? You're transforming.

Progress is success. Moving even a millimeter beyond where you were yesterday is a triumph. So, show up. Push through. Each tiny improvement, each small victory, is proof that you're evolving. **Follow-through is not just an act—it's a declaration of success.** You only truly fail when you stop trying. Every single moment you decide to push through, no matter how small the step, you're already successful.

4. Practicing The Mindset of Giving Back: Unlocking Abundance Through Service

"Generally speaking, the most miserable people I know are those who are obsessed with themselves; the happiest people I know are those who lose themselves in the service of others... By and large, I have come to see that if we complain about life, it is because we are thinking only of ourselves," said Gordon B. Hinckley. And he's right. A selfish life is a miserable one—not because

it's wrong to care about yourself, but because humans simply aren't wired for isolation or self-absorption.

We thrive on connection, on helping others, and on being part of something bigger than ourselves. When you help others, something extraordinary happens: you create genuine bonds and connections that make life richer and more meaningful. Neuroscience even backs this up. Acts of kindness trigger the release of **oxytocin, serotonin, and dopamine**—hormones that elevate your mood, increase feelings of love and connection, and actively block cortisol (the stress hormone). If you're looking for a way to combat depression, loneliness, or dissatisfaction with life, this is it: **serve others, and in doing so, you'll find yourself.**

The beauty of service is that it doesn't require grand gestures. Start small:

- **Listen** to a friend who's struggling.
- **Smile** at a stranger on the street.
- **Donate** a little money or time to someone who is less fortunate.
- **Offer help** to someone who needs your help.

These simple acts of kindness might seem trivial, but their impact on your emotional state is profound. With every act of giving, you'll notice a lightness in your body and a deep satisfaction in your soul. The happiness you feel isn't fleeting—it's the natural reward for doing what we're designed to do: care for each other.

True mastery extends beyond personal gain; it encompasses the desire to uplift others. When your focus shifts from just "getting" to "giving," you unlock an entirely new level of fulfillment and abundance. As you practice kindness, you are taking yourself to the next level, whether by volunteering, mentoring, or simply being a reliable source of love and support for those around you. Success is hollow without contribution, but when you build your life around serving others, you tap into a deeper purpose.

Mastery is not about reaching a destination but about cultivating the elements that allow you to navigate life's journey with resilience, clarity, and purpose. Faith roots you in strength, an organized mind gives you clarity, decisiveness ignites action, follow-through builds consistency, and a spirit of giving unlocks fulfillment. When you integrate all these elements into your life, you don't just live—you thrive. You've built the foundation for living a life of mastery.

Living In the New Me

But remember, mastery is in the daily choices. It's in how you choose to approach each moment—with purpose, presence, and a desire to serve. Let your faith guide you, your actions be intentional, and your heart remain open. When these pillars align, success is not just a destination—it becomes the very essence of who you are.

As we come to the final pages of this book, I want to express my deepest gratitude to you—the reader, my unseen companion on this journey of transformation. Though we may never meet, our spirits are connected, walking together toward a better, brighter future.

I believe in you. You are uniquely gifted, talented, and irreplaceable. You were brought to this earth with a special mission that only you can fulfill. No one else can create or achieve what you're here to do. That is your superpower, your divine purpose.

Whenever you feel lonely, lost, confused, or weak, I urge you to return to this book. Let these pages remind you of your infinite potential and serve as a guiding light in your darkest moments. Embrace the rituals, habits, and practices within these chapters—not just once, but as an integral part of your everyday life.

Your New Self

Your life is waiting to unfold in ways you can't yet imagine. It is brimming with beauty, success, and love—all uniquely crafted for you, by you.

Final Words

"I dream of a day when the potential of married couples in this country can be unleashed for the good of humankind, when husbands and wives live life with full emotional love tanks and reach out to accomplish their potential as individuals and as couples. I dream of a day when children can grow up in homes filled with love and security, where children's developing energies can be channeled to learn and serving rather than seeking the love they did not receive at home" —Gary Chapman

AS I CLOSE this chapter, I am overwhelmed with a sense of love, abundance, and deep connection. My heart feels wide open, as if it's physically expanding with each breath I take, filled with gratitude for this journey I've walked. It's a journey I hope you will join, not just for the betterment of yourself but for the ripple effect it will have on the world around you.

This book is my invitation to you to walk that path—to reflect on who you are, to nurture your faith and virtue, to be deliberate in building a life rooted in balance, love, and intentionality. We are not meant to live lives of quiet desperation, bound by fear or disconnected from our true purpose. The **universe wants us to thrive**, to be rich not just in material wealth but in spiritual fulfillment. We are surrounded by abundance—the sun's energy, the earth's water, the food we are given. These resources have always been here, sustaining us since birth. But true richness is when we tap into the **deep wellspring of our potential**, align with our higher selves, and live with an open heart.

It's easy to lose our way in the noise of modern life, in the distractions of technology, in the race for external achievements. But if you stop and look around, you'll notice that **nature has never lost its way**. The trees still grow, the rivers still flow, and the sun still rises, following a rhythm that's existed long before us. We are no different. The answers to happiness, to fulfillment, are already embedded within us. We just need to **return to our roots**, to listen to the whispers of nature, and to align ourselves with the deeper inner truths of life.

In every setback, in every challenge, there is a hidden gift—a lesson that is guiding you closer to your true path. Trust that the universe is working in your favor, and know that you are exactly where you need to be. With

Final Words

each small act of faith, with each moment of virtue, you are building something greater than yourself.

This journey is not about perfection; it's about progress. It's about waking up each day with the intention to grow, to love, to give, and to live fully. When we live in alignment with these truths, we not only transform our own lives but also inspire those around us to do the same. This is how we change the world—one heart, one family, one community at a time.

As I finish writing this book, I am filled with excitement for what comes next, both for myself and for you. I truly believe that the universe has great things in store for all of us. May this book be the spark that lights the fire of transformation within you, and may you carry that light with you wherever you go.

In the end, we are all just **walking each other home**, back to the place of love, faith, and abundance that we were always meant to live in. Let's continue this journey together. Let's create a world where everyone lives with full hearts, fulfilled potential, and boundless joy.

The path is here before you. All you have to do is take the first step.

www.ingramcontent.com/pod-product-compliance
Lightning Source LLC
Chambersburg PA
CBHW032223080426
42735CB00008B/690